365 Bedtime Horse Tales

text: Francisca Fröhlich
illustrations: Maan Jansen

Copyright © 1997 by Rebo International b.v., Lisse, The Netherlands

This 2005 edition published by Backpack Books, by arrangement
with Rebo International b.v.

Backpack Books
122 Fifth Avenue
New York, NY 10011

ISBN 0-7607-7270-3

Printed and bound in Slovenia

05 06 07 08 09 MCH 10 9 8 7 6 5 4 3 2 1

Text: Francisca Fröhlich
Cover design: AdAm Studio, Prague, The Czech Republic
Translation: Stephen Challacombe, Hastings, Great Britain
Typesetting: Hof&Land Typografie, Maarssen, The Netherlands
Prepress services: AdAm Studio, Prague, The Czech Republic
Proofreading: Emily Sands, Eva Munk and Karen Taschek

365 Bedtime Horse Tales

text: Francisca Fröhlich
illustrations: Maan Jansen

BACK**PACK**BOOKS
○
NEW YORK

January 1

Snow

Huge snowflakes are falling and lying on the grass in the big meadow. It is really, really cold out-of-doors. Because it is so cold and raw, there is nobody to be seen.
Nobody? Actually, there is someone. Here comes Tim. He opens the gate and goes to fetch his pony.
Clip, clop go the pony's hooves. The pony doesn't mind the weather. She has a thick blanket to protect her against the cold and snow. Tim quickly lets the pony loose.
Immediately she gallops away from Tim. Just to the end of the field and then she gallops back again. Look, here she comes again with mane streaming as she gallops. She nuzzles Tim and is off again. It's such fun to rush around in the snow.

January 2

Forgotten

Oh! It has suddenly got so cold. It is already getting dark. Ruthy, the brown pony, is by the gate. She is waiting for her owner. He comes every evening to collect her and to take her to a nice warm stable. Where is he?
Ruthy peers and peers for him until her eyes start to smart.
Surely her owner, Chubby John, could not forget her?
But then she is happy to see him coming on his bike.
"Hi, Ruthy!" calls the well-known voice.
"Are you coming with me?" What a silly question.
Of course Ruthy is going to go with him.
Because not only is the stable lovely and warm,
there are also scrumptious pony treats waiting.

Peppermint

Dobbin is the pig food man's horse. Every day he must haul the cart for his master through the streets of the town. It's okay when they start, because the cart is empty. But then, there is a bucket full of scraps at almost every house. Potato peelings, vegetable waste and sometimes stale bread and old fruit. Dobbin's boss is not very well off. Yet he looks after Dobbin as best he can. Dobbin gets hay and some oats. And at the end of the trip, he gets a reward. Can you guess what it is? A delicious peppermint. Dobbin is nuts about peppermints. Crunch, crunch goes the mint as he chews it. But a peppermint is not very big. Dobbin eats it up immediately. Then he has to wait until the next evening. "What a shame," whinnies Dobbin.

January 4

Emma

Emma is five years old. She goes to preschool,
but otherwise she would rather stay at home
with Mommy. Emma enjoys being at home.
She can help Mommy with the vacuuming and
the shopping. The best day of the week is
Wednesday. Because on Wednesday the pig
food man comes to their street. An hour before
he is due, Emma waits at the window. She scans
the street for the pig food man's horse.
"Mommy, Mommy, he's coming!" she shrieks.
While Mommy empties the bucket of peelings
and scrapings onto the cart, Emma gives the
horse a carrot. The pig food man always waits
until his horse has eaten the carrot before he
moves on. "Bye, horsey," calls Emma.
"Until next week!"

January 5

The winter fair

It is usually very quiet in the town square. In the winter, people are usually indoors in front of the fire. But nobody is staying indoors today. The fair is here. The winter fair. The entire town square is decorated brightly and filled with stalls. Grandma came to pick Ben up immediately after lunch. They go to the fair together.

"What do you want to do, Ben?" asks Grandma.

Ben nods. "I want to ride on the merry-go-around."

They are in luck. There are two merry-go-rounds at the fair. One very modern one with cars, motorcycles and even a rocket. And a really traditional one with horses. Granny thinks Ben wants to ride in a bright shiny race car. But Ben only has eyes for the horses. He wants to spend the whole afternoon riding around and around on such a beautiful wooden horse.

January 6

Around and around

"Giddyup! Giddyup, horsey, gallop!"
Jabbing heels and banging stirrups,
Ben urges the wooden pony on.
Going around and around is such fun.
"Hey, Mister Merry-go-around Man,
Another ride, oh please, please, Gran."
Instead the merry-go-around starts to slow,
Ben's eyes fill with so much woe.
Granny has a big, broad smile,
"Okay, Ben, just a little while."
Grandma pays the man once more.
Ben's horse rises up out of the floor,
Up and down, and around and around
Ben can see the roofs across the town.
But when his horse begins to slow,
It's "please, please, Granny, one more go."

Giant

Farmer Hagley has just bought Prince, and now everyone is laughing at him. "What are you going to do with such a giant? He will eat you out of house and home. You can't even ride him!" Prince is actually a heavy horse. He has an enormous head, four strong legs and the hindquarters of an elephant. Farmer Hagley takes no notice of the scorn. He draws himself up and says: "I think Prince is the best looking horse I've ever seen. What's more, he's got a lovely nature. That's good enough for me." Prince is also happy with his lot. Prince is becoming very attached to Farmer Hagley. When the people laugh at him he thinks: Just wait, the day will come when I'll prove myself.

January 8

Clock

Farmer Hagley's farm is right on the edge of town. Every morning a large yellow school bus drives past. The bus takes the children from the neighborhood to school in the town. Farmer Hagley's giant draft horse, Prince, likes to watch the yellow bus. This morning he stands waiting near the fence next to the road as usual. But the bus is late – far too late. Perhaps you wonder how Prince can know. After all, horses can't tell time.

But Prince has a clock in his tummy that keeps perfect time. He knows when it is seven in the morning. That's when the farmer takes him out of the stable. He also knows when it is time to be put back in the stable each evening. He is always waiting by the gate. Prince also knows that the bus comes past at ten past eight. He knows too that it is now much later than that, and the bus still is not here.

January 9

To the rescue

The eyes of the children pop out at the sight. It is so unusual. Some of their school friends live on a farm. They come to school by bus every day. But today the roads are icy and slippery. The bus cannot run. Driving is far too dangerous. Yet those children from the country have come to school! They have been brought by Farmer Hagley. He has put his big strong draft horse between the shafts of a cart and brought all the children from his neighborhood to school. Prince has special horseshoes so that he does not slip.
What fun that was! The town children are jealous.
They too would like to ride in Prince's cart.

15

Patchwork pony

Horses come in all sorts of colors. There are dark brown and jet black horses. There are chestnut horses with blond manes, and there are dappled grays. Esther's horse is all kinds of colors. Her body is covered with brown patches, black patches, white patches and some gray here and there. Guess what Esther calls her pony. She calls her Patch.

"Yes," laughs Esther, "she looks like a patchwork pony."

Patch is quite happy with her name. She does not mind being called a patchwork pony.

"That makes me very special," she whinnies.

"No other horse in the world looks like me."

January 11

George and Jimmy

George and Jimmy are two Shetland ponies. They have stout heads, rounded bellies and short legs. Now that it is winter, they have also grown a thick coat of hair. Because of their coats they are not troubled by the cold.

Even when it snows, George and Jimmy go outside.

"Whee-hee-heee," cries George, galloping through the meadow.

"Wait for me!" calls Jimmy, racing pell-mell after his brother. But it has snowed heavily. A thick, white blanket covers the field.

"This isn't fun anymore," grumbles George.

"No," agreed Jimmy.

His little legs sink right into the snow.

They quickly trot back to their warm stable.

January 12

Sleigh

It has been freezing so long that it crunches underfoot. There is a thick layer of ice on the ditches and drainage channels. Ormand, the black Friesian heavy horse stallion, stamps impatiently in his stall. He knows that today is the great day. Today he will go on the ice. First he must be shod with special horseshoes. Then his master takes him to a wide channel. The sleigh awaits Ormand.
Ormand finds it takes far too long to put him between the shafts. He wants to trot in front of the sleigh. He wants to stretch his long, black legs. Finally everything is ready. His master has no need to crack the whip. Ormand trots off immediately. There goes the sleigh over the ice. "Good riddance to that stupid stable!" whinnies Ormand. "I'm not going back. I'll stay on the ice."
But what will you do, Ormand, when it thaws?

January 13

Frozen

Life for a horse is not always fun, especially in the winter. You become quite stiff if you must spend the whole day in a stable. But if you must go out into the field when it is freezing, that is also not so nice. Particularly if the water in the drinking trough is frozen. That's why Beth has taken a ball with her down to her pony Bonita's field. The ball is to float in the water to stop it freezing. But silly Bonita does not know that. The pony thinks the ball is to play with. Time and again she knocks it out with her nose and kicks it with her hoof.
Silly, silly Bonita. Soon your water will be frozen again.

Surprise

Annette is crazy about horses. Sometimes she is taken to the children's farm. If the weather is fine, she is allowed to ride the ponies there. Most of all Annette would like her own pony. But Mommy and Daddy think she is still too small. Annette doesn't think that's fair.

"Now that it's winter, we never ever go to the children's farm," she grumbles. Mommy and Daddy find that a bit sad for Annette. That's why they have a surprise for her. When Annette wakes up in the morning, there is a huggable little pony in her room. Not a real horse, but a rocking horse.

"Now you can practice for the summer," says Daddy. "For when the children's farm opens up again."

January 15

Grooming

Now that it is so cold and raw outside, Whisky the horse spends the whole day in her stable. She nibbles her hay a little and paces to and fro.

"Thank goodness I've got a big stable," sighs Whisky. "But I'd rather be in the field. Galloping and jumping out-of-doors is much more fun."

Fortunately, her owner comes to see her every day. And every day the brushes are brought out. Her owner grooms her completely until she is really clean.

"Mmm! That's nice!" Whisky whickers appreciatively. The brush scratches splendidly in all those places that itch.

"Scratch my back again!" whinnies a contented Whisky. "I can't reach there myself."

January 16

Hunger

The horses stand pitifully in the field. It is cold and wet and the wind is blowing very hard. The horses cluster closely together. This keeps them a little bit warmer. To take their minds off the cold, they tell each other nice things.

"If I shut my eyes I see a meadow full of tender grass," says one horse.

"And I see a trough full of pony treats and a rack full of hay," says the other.

"Shut up!" says the third horse.

All this talk of food is making my tummy rumble. Now I'm not just cold. I'm hungry too!"

"Be quiet," says the second horse again, "I see the bright sun high in the sky. It is just like a fire on my coat. I'm so warm that I want to jump into the stream!"

20

Vitamins

Elsie Holm bikes to school every day. On the way, she passes a field with three horses in it. In the summer, the horses gambol happily in the grass. But in the winter, they stand looking rather dejected.

Elsie sympathizes with the horses. That's why she has bought a big bag of carrots with her pocket money. This morning she stops by the fence to the field. She puts her fingers to her mouth and whistles loudly through her fingers. Three horse heads look up. What does the girl want?

Let's have a look. What a surprise! The girl pulls three large carrots from her jacket pocket.

"Eat them up," says Elsie. "We all need extra vitamins in the winter."

January 18

A-tishoo

Ajax the large farm horse is really naughty. He is always up to tricks. He wiggles the door to his stable open with his sensitive lips. And then Ajax goes exploring.
"This smells of hay!" Ajax follows his nose.
Oh dear! Ajax has found the haystack and enjoys rolling on the ground. But the hay is dry and full of dust. Tickle, tickle go Ajax's nostrils.
"A-ah-ahhh-tishooo!" And once more: "A-tishoo."
Ajax cannot stop sneezing. Poor Ajax – but he did bring it on himself.

January 19

Stuck-up

Pussy cat Thomasina is looking for a nice warm spot to take a nap. She knows that it is nice and warm in the horse's stable. That's why she slips in through a window and jumps slap into the stall of Ali the Arab.
Startled, Ali angrily noses the cat.
"What are you doing?" he neighs in annoyance. "Get out of my stall, lowlife."
"Now, now, dear heart," meows Thomasina. "Surely I can share the warmth of the stable. It is cold outside and I am an animal, just like you."
"Pfff!" Ali blasts air through his lips. "As if cats were as important as horses. Don't make me laugh! Cats are not noble animals – horses are. So I'm not going to share my stable with you!"
What a stuck-up beast!

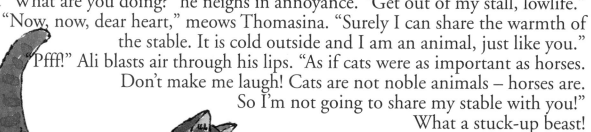

January 20

Noble animal

Ali the Arab is a very proud horse. He cost a lot of money and he knows it! Ali looks down on other animals.
"All animals have legs, but a horse has limbs," he says conceitedly. " And they have a head, but I have a profile. I am a noble animal."
Ali looks in the water of his drinking trough. The water acts as a mirror.
"Oh, how beautiful I am!" sighs Ali. To see better, he bends his head closer to the water.
Plop, he sticks his nose right in the water. Ali sneezes.
Now he has a noble attack of the sneezes.

January 21

Carrots

Carrots are very tasty and what's more, they are good for you. Even a really big carrot slips easily into a horse's mouth.
"Pffworr, what a tiny snack!" The horse shakes his great head.
"I would like another piece, but the carrot is all gone."

Loathing

Anna does horse riding and gymnastics. Riding is the best thing she can imagine, but she finds gymnastics awful. Unfortunately she has a bad back, which is why the doctor has ordered her to do gymnastics.

"Otherwise you can forget about riding, young lady," the doctor says. Every Thursday afternoon finds Anna in a bad mood in the changing room. "Gym is so boring. It's much nicer working with horses," she moans through her teeth. The gym teacher hears her.

"Do you really want to work with a horse? That's possible here too."

Anna cannot believe her ears.

"Is that really true?" Immediately she pulls her gym clothes on.

"Horse" works like magic on Anna.

January 23

Strange horse

Anna walks into the gymnasium. Her teacher says that today she can work with a horse. Anna's curiosity is really aroused about that horse. Has the teacher borrowed a horse from the riding stables?

But in the gymnasium there is a strange apparatus. It has four legs topped by leather-covered padding.

"How do you like my horse?" laughs the gym teacher.

"Is that a horse?" Anna points at the apparatus.

"Yes, that is my horse. It is the nicest horse in the world. It doesn't kick, doesn't bite and most of all, it doesn't need feeding.

And it doesn't mind if you jump on its back," jokes the teacher. Anna laughs too. The gym teacher has really fooled her.

Black Beauty

Before the riding lesson the children are allowed to choose the pony they want to ride. Most of the children have a favorite pony. Dan too has his favorite. Dan is a rather brash young man with a strong country accent. The riding teacher asks Dan which horse he prefers.
"And which one do you want, Dan?" she asks.
"I want to ride Bootie," Dan replies with determination.
"Bootie? Bootie? We haven't got a horse called Bootie," says a surprised teacher.
Dan points to the stable housing a beautiful black pony.
"Oh, you mean Black Beauty!" grasps the teacher. "Yes," says Dan. "That's what I said, Black Bootie."

January 25

Whip

Arabella has a real hatred of whips. Once she sees one she begins to buck. That's why the children ride her without a whip. But Sarah has just gotten a lovely new whip for her birthday.
"I don't care, I'm going to try it out," says the headstrong young girl as she climbs onto Arabella. At first Arabella is calm. It looks as though she isn't going to react to the whip today. But then she bucks ferociously. Sarah needs both hands to hang on. The whip falls to the ground. Arabella pounds down upon the lovely new whip. *Crack,* goes the whip as it breaks in two.
"Teach you to be so headstrong," neighs Arabella.

Sniffles

Clara is a bit worried when she looks at her horse this morning.
Nicky is looking rather glum and hangs her head. There are streams of white
mucus running from the horse's nostrils. "Oh, Nicky!" cries Clara.
"I hope you're not really ill."
"No, dear, Nicky isn't seriously ill. But she does have a cold," Clara's mom
reassures her. "You must pamper her lots and give her extra vitamins.
She'll soon be herself again." Clara nods.
When she has a cold, Mommy really looks after her.
"Mommy, do you have a dish towel?" she asks.
"A dish towel?" Mommy asks in surprise.
Clara nods again. "An ordinary hankie would be of no use to blow Nicky's nose."

January 27

Hard work

If you have your own pony, you will always be busy.
The stable has to be mucked out and your pony groomed.
The manure has to be picked up out of the field and you must prepare the feed.
And then you need to clean and oil the saddle and harness from time to time,
or they will not last.
Linda has her own horse. Faithfully she does all the jobs because she is crazy about
her horse. She's in the stable every day mucking out.
When she wheels a barrow full of manure, she finds herself saying:
"Gosh, what a lot of manure from one horse!"
But when her horse nuzzles her neck, Linda forgets all the hard work.

January 28

Winter pony

January brings the winter snow,
Oh, how the cold winds blow!
Yet they do not trouble pony Rex.
How warmly my thick coat protects,
Even though I've icicles on mane and tail
And nothing but ice in my water pail.
Because my breed is really tough,
I frolic and play and kick this stuff.

January 29

Blanket

When it is cold outdoors, Effy gets a blanket. The blanket is fastened over her back by straps tied under her belly. There are also straps attached to her hind legs to keep the blanket in place. It does not move, not even when Effy rolls on the ground. But today one of the straps on the hind legs has broken free. When Effy walks, the strap is trailed on the ground. Grrrt, grrrt!
Effy is startled. She thinks there is someone behind her. She leaps around but nobody is there. But when she takes another step or two she hears it again: grrrt, grrrrt.
"Now I've got you!" she neighs, turning around again. She keeps doing this over and over again. Poor, silly Effy turns around and around. I hope her mistress soon comes to fix the strap. Otherwise Effy will get dizzy.

January 30

Plaits

Today is the day of the show. Hannah the pony is trampling her stable floor.
Look, here comes Lucy, her rider. Lucy has a plastic bag with her.
There is a comb and lots of hair bands in it.
Hannah has to be made beautiful for the show.
Her mane and tail must be combed and plaited.
Lucy combs Hannah's mane carefully. She then plaits small tufts of hair and fastens
them with a hair band. It is lots of work.
Lucy is busy for at least half an hour but finally Hannah is ready.
"Look, Hannah, how beautiful you look." Lucy takes a mirror from the bag and
holds it in front of Hannah's nose. But Hannah does not know what a mirror is
for.
She thinks it is something to eat and she tries to bite it.
"No one could call you vain," laughs Lucy.

28

Two big, black horse's eyes

Two big, black horse's eyes
Look on with anticipation.
"Are we going for an outing today?
Will it be joy and jubilation,
Or grooming with brush and comb
If so, I hope she finds that itch
That I can't reach to scratch.
But who on earth's this little witch?"

Two small, caring child's hands
Gently stroke the horse's nose.
The little girl is so tiny that
She must stand on tippy-toes.
Ten loving child's fingers
Caress the horse so tenderly.
In reply, the horse bends its head
And nuzzles the girl gingerly.

February 1

Coffee

If you ask Bella, the heavy draft horse, what the tastiest thing in the world is, she answers: "Coffee."

That may sound rather strange. But you must know that from first thing in the morning until late in the evening, Bella works hard for her master. The entire day is spent hauling logs and tree trunks out of the woods. The only rest Bella gets is when her boss takes a break. When that happens, he unscrews the lid of his thermos.

Once Bella smells coffee she knows she can take it easy.

"Mmmmm," sniffs Bella. "I've never tried it, but coffee is definitely the tastiest thing in the whole wide world."

February 2

Dappled

None of the other children can stand Derek.

He sticks his nose in everywhere.

In the stable he checks how the others are grooming their ponies.

"You've missed a bit!" or, "Have you cleaned out the hooves?" and,

"There's a bit of straw in the tail."

During the lesson, he pays more attention to what the other children are doing than to his own gray pony.

When Derek is a nuisance, the other children just shrug.

"Take no notice of him," they say, "He talks big. His pony may be dappled, but he's plain dumb, stupid. That's why we call him Dopey Derek."

February 3

Nappy

Long ago, before there were cars, many coaches were driven through the town. Katy's grandpa used to have a taxi firm – or rather a hackney carriage company. Grandpa tells of those days.

"Everything was better then," he says. "There weren't any exhaust fumes from horses. There was fresh air on the streets."

"Yes, but surely, Gramps…horses poop. It can't have been so nice with all those horse droppings on the street. You could step in it when crossing the road."

Grandpa shakes his head. "Horse manure doesn't smell unpleasant. It is natural. Besides, my horses had a bag over their tail to catch their droppings. Once the bag was full, I emptied it on the manure heap."

"What a laugh," whooped Katy. "So your horses wore diapers."

February 4

Alone

It's lonely alone,
Everyone knows that!
In this great field all on my own,
With no one to play with or whinny at.
Life's such a bore, so empty now
With nothing to do but eat and sleep.
No company except the big black crow.
Even that scarce makes a peep,
Except "craw, craw" off and on.
Ah well, let's go to sleep.

February 5

A friend

Since Danny Boy has been with Angela, the pony is very sad. He is missing his friends from the stables where he used to live. Now all alone, he stands in a field looking over the fence. He stares at the road. Perhaps some horses will pass by. But only cars drive that way. Angela sympathizes with Danny Boy. She knows he is lonely. But Daddy has said that one pony costs enough, so there can be no pony friend for Danny Boy. Yet Angela's dad solves the problem. He buys a sweet little goat at the market. It can keep Danny Boy company in his field.
Danny Boy first views the new arrival with suspicion, but when the goat springs into the air, he thinks, I can do that too.
The two of them dart around the meadow together. Danny Boy is no longer lonely.

Attila

Attila is a stalwart stallion. He is the leader of the herd and makes sure everyone knows it. If the others will not obey, he shows his teeth.

"Watch it!" he whinnies at them. "Do what I tell you."

Then up he rears and gallops around. "Nobody's as powerful as me."

"Tchaa, what a braggart," mumble the rest of the horses.

They have absolutely no interest in all that business. It is hard enough to find sufficient food to eat in the winter.

That is why they let Attila play the boss. "He'll soon learn his lesson," they mutter knowingly.

February 7

Storm

"Whooo-oo-ooooh," whines the wind over the ground. The trees and bushes bend before the storm. The horses can barely find any shelter. That is why they stand together for protection from the sweeping wind.

But where is Attila, that stalwart stallion? He is so strong and so brave, isn't he? Why is he not protecting the herd?

If you look carefully, you can see Attila's ears, right in the center of the group of horses. His ears are shaking with fear.

"Phooey," laughs Larka the mare. "A little bit of wind and our brave stallion is terrified! And he wants to lead the herd? Such a coward!"

February 8

Panic

When Sally arrives at the riding school that
afternoon, she notices something is wrong.
"Have you heard?" asks another girl, "Samantha
has gone."
What? Sally is shocked. Samantha gone?
It cannot be true.
Samantha is her favorite pony.
She is always good and despite her twenty-two
years, she still worked every lesson with the
children.
Sally immediately runs to Samantha's stall.
When she sees that it is empty, she panics. Sally
once heard than when horses get too old to work
they go to the dog food company. She always
thought it was just a story.
But faced now with Samantha's empty stable,
she is worried it might be true.
Tears well in her eyes and flow in torrents down
her cheeks.
Samantha must not become horse meat!

February 9

In retirement

Angry and upset, Sally runs to the owner of the riding school.
"Why have you sent Samantha to be made into dog food?" she screams. The
owner is taken aback. "Dog food? You silly girl! Samantha now has a lovely new
home.
She is too old to be ridden all the time. That's why I have been looking for ages to
find a good home for her.
Now she can spend the entire day in a field if she likes and she will be well fed. She
will still be ridden occasionally, but otherwise, she is retired."
Fresh tears pour from Sally's eyes.
But this time they are tears of joy.
Samantha lives! She has truly earned her retirement!

Apple for the thirst

Billy stands in his box, waiting and snorting.
It is breakfast time. Where is his owner?
Oh, here he comes. His master gives him fresh water, fresh hay and some pony treats in his trough every morning. And in the winter, he gets a fresh apple.
"That's another treat," says his master.
Billy immediately attacks the feed. He eats the hay and the pony treats, and he drinks the water with his tongue. Only the apple is left. Perhaps you think Billy does not like apples. That is not so. In fact, he is crazy about them. That is why he saves them.
"If I need something later," he neighs, "I will still have an apple to quench my thirst."

February 11

Big belly

Rosy the mare is getting fatter and fatter. Her saddle does not fit anymore and the girth will almost not go around her huge belly.

"I don't understand it," says Mark. "Rosy doesn't get any more to eat than the others." Rosy keeps her thoughts to herself. Silly Mark. Doesn't he realize that last summer she met a nice young colt? The two of them spent several weeks in a field together. That's how foals are created! There has been a foal growing in her belly since last summer.

"Just wait, Mark," she whinnies softly. "In a month or two, I will have a big surprise for you."

February 12

Jab

All horses get an injections against horse illnesses. The vet comes with a huge syringe. Rollo the pony does not like injections. When he hears the vet's truck, he creeps into the rear corner of his stable.

"Come on, Rollo. Surely you're not afraid of one little prick?" asks the vet.

"Go away!" Rollo hisses through his teeth, rearing and bucking. He has already decided not to give the vet a chance this year. He keeps his eye peeled for the syringe.

"It's a clever man who can manage to stick me," he snorts. The vet shakes his head.

"What a stubborn pony. He will be ill for certain."

Be ill? Rollo doesn't want that.

"If that jab can prevent me from getting ill, go ahead then!"

February 13

Tick tock tick

Hey – what is that? Cissie whinnies in surprise. It is the middle of the night and there is a deathly hush everywhere. All the other horses are sleeping, but not Cissie. She has heard something – tick, tock, tick – very softly in her stable. She takes a few careful steps and sniffs something in the hay with her nose. Tick, tock, tick – she can hear it clearly now. "Oh, it's a watch. It must belong to the man who grooms me so thoroughly. Won't he be pleased when I give it back to him!" Cissie tries to pick it up with her hoof, but a watch cannot withstand a hoof. Crack! Will the man still be pleased Cissie found his watch?

February 14

Hurry up

When the entire winter has to be spent in a stable, a horse longs for the open field. That is why it is wonderful to be let out on a fine winter day.

"Hee-ee-eeee," cries Robin excitedly.

He tries hard to walk patiently beside his owner, who takes him to the meadow. He cannot wait until the gate is opened. He tramples the ground with his hoof and pushes with his nose while his master fiddles with the catch of the gate.

"Hee-ee-ee! Hurry up!"

"Robin!" shouts his owner angrily. "Stop shoving. I will never it get it open if you act up. Watch out or I'll take you back to your stable!"

Robin is beyond control. He jerks himself free, takes a run up and…jumps over the fence.

"Hee-ee-ee, that's the way," he whinnies boisterously as he gallops off.

February 15

Impatience

If you're a young horse,
Barely seven years old.
There's no time for patience
Or listening to what you're told.
At seven years old, it's asking far
too much
To obediently follow master.
Instead it's pull against the rein
And say, "Can't we go much
faster?"

39

February 16

Martin

Martin is a Fjord pony. He is very fond of his owner, but he likes eating even more. Martin is strong and sturdy and can easily stand the winter out-of-doors. During the day he can stay in the field, even in the winter. In the evening, Mark comes to collect him to take him back to the stable. Martin usually doesn't want to go.
"I haven't eaten all the grass yet," he whickers.
But Mark knows Martin's weakness. He knows how much the horse likes eating. He dangles a carrot. "Hmmmph," trumpets Martin.
"Carrots are tastier than grass shoots." Martin has worked that out.
While Martin happily chews the carrot, Mark leads him to the stable.

School play

The teacher has a surprise for the children at school.

"Girls and boys," she calls, clapping her hands. "In a few weeks, the school will be ten years old."

"Hooray! A party? What fun!" scream the children. The teacher nods.

"And to celebrate, our class is going to put on a play."

"Yippee! Hooray!"

This appeals to the children even more. Every child wants a part in the play – preferably the leading role.

"We'll start by allocating the parts," says Miss.

"There is a role for everybody, so no one will be left out."

With great curiosity, the children wait to see what part they will play.

Wonder horse

The teacher distributes all the parts in the school play. Wendy is to be the princess and Tom the king. Jimmy is the villain and Stephen the policeman. Lots of the children are to act as townspeople. Henry wants to be the farmer. Now there are just two children without parts, Lizzie and Daphne.

"I've kept the most difficult roles for you two," laughs the teacher. She knows the girls are both crazy about horse riding. "You girls together are to play Trojan the wonder horse."

Daphne and Lizzie look puzzled. How can they both play a horse? Then the teacher shows them the horse costume. It is marvelous. Daphne crawls into the front end and Lizzie into the rear. Lizzie has to grab Daphne by the waist and the teacher zips up the costume.

"He-ee-eee!" screams Daphne, beginning to trot.

"Hey, careful!" shouts the belly of the horse. "Not so fast!"

February 19

Cowboy

If you ask Nick what he wants to be when he grows up, he answers with certainty: "I want to be a cowboy."

Nick is nuts about cowboy movies. He thinks the rugged men are amazing. They ride for months through wild terrain on their horses. Nick thinks that's fantastic. He has a length of rope at home. That is his lasso. The banister is his horse and an old cushion is his saddle.

"Ya-hoo!" shouts Nick, seated on the banister as he kicks his heels to spur it on. "Yaa-hooo," Nick swirls his lasso.

"Crack!" answers the banister, collapsing under him. "Ouch!" cries Nick as he counts his bruises. Oh well, a cowboy's life is full of danger, Nick has found.

February 20

Birthday

Mary's pony, Fran, has her birthday today. Mary has decided there must be a real birthday party. She gets streamers and balloons from the cupboard. She will decorate Fran's stable with them.

"Happy birthday to you, happy birthday to you…" sings Mary as she enters the stable. Fran pricks her ears. Mary sings beautifully.

"Many happy returns, Fran," Mary says, cuddling her pony. "Many happy returns." Fran does not understand any of it. Horses know nothing about birthdays. When Mary tries to hang up the streamers, the horse tugs them so hard that they fall down right onto her neck.

"So you'd rather wear them around your neck?" laughs Mary. "That's an even better idea."

February 21

Snack

Anna has seen her sister Mary taking streamers to Fran's stable. "Of course, it's Fran's birthday!" she shrieks. Now, Anna is just as crazy about Fran as Mary. So she too wants to mark the birthday somehow. But how? What do you do for a birthday? Anna has an idea. Flowers! Except where do you find flowers in the middle of the winter? Fortunately, Anna remembers that Mommy has placed a vase with flowers in the front room. Mommy won't mind if I borrow them until tomorrow, thinks Anna.

With the bunch of flowers in her arms, she heads to the stable.

"He-ee!" whinnies Fran. "That's better than streamers. After all, flowers can be eaten. Glump!" In one bite, the flowers are gone. Dear, oh dear, how is Anna going to explain this to Mommy?

February 22

Sandy rider

Susie has recently started taking riding lessons,
Today she is allowed to join the others for the
first time. Nervously she climbs on her pony
with an eye on the teacher. If she listens
carefully, everything will be all right.
"Now remember," bellows Miss Simkins. "Pay
attention, everyone. I don't want any sandy
riders during my lesson."
"Sandy riders?" Susie is worried. "What does she
mean?" Just to be sure, she dismounts and
brushes and beats her clothes and hair to make
sure there is absolutely no grain of sand on her.
Certain there are none, she climbs back in the
saddle.
"Now I'm not a sandy rider," she laughs. Her
pony shakes its head. Silly Susie doesn't know
what a sandy rider is. Hang on, her pony will
soon show her. He bucks suddenly and – oops!
There is Susie in the sand.
"There," snickers her pony. "Now you really
now what a sandy rider is."

February 23

An elephant's memory

It is often said that an elephant never forgets. However old they become, they
know precisely who has been nice to them and those who were not. Charlie Girl
the horse can match an elephant for memory. Ages ago she belonged to a man who
always hit and kicked her. Happily she was sold one day to a sweet girl who takes
good care of her. The girl is called Zoë.
Together, they often go for country rides, which they both enjoy. Except that when
they ride close to Charlie Girl's former owner, she becomes nervous. Then she is
quite uncontrollable and wants to get past as quickly as possible. Zoë therefore
decides to take a different route.
"You can't help having a memory like an elephant," she tells Charlie Girl, as she
pats her neck.

44

Nasty man

Hey, look! It's that nasty man,
Who hits horses every chance he can.
He thinks that's how to train a horse.
Just proves he's an idiot, of course.

Anyone with half a brain
Must surely know that you can't train
An animal as big as me,
Unless you gain my sympathy.

A kind word, a gentle hand,
From the nicest mistress in this land,
Make me much more keen and eager
To try so hard to really please her.

A trip

Carla has lived her entire life with Farmer Ventress. That may seem a long time, but Carla is only one year old. She was born last spring and since then she has been down in the meadow with the other foals darting about and playing. Farmer Ventress takes good care of his foals, not just because he loves horses. They can also earn him lots of money.

Once a year he takes some of the foals to the horse market. Usually he manages to sell them all and returns home with an empty trailer and a full wallet.

Carla does not know this, of course. When she sees the truck and trailer drive up, she thinks: "Hey, we are going on a trip."

The horse market

There are lots of people at the horse market. There are people who wish to sell horses and others who wish to buy them. There are also lots of people who just watch what is going on.
Carla watches everything with open eyes.
She has never seen so many people. Why are they all here?
A young boy comes running over to Carla.
"Daddy, Daddy, look! What a lovely foal!" calls the boy as he strokes Carla's nose.
"Hee-ee, master!" calls Carla.
"Look what a nice young boy."

February 27

Shake hands

Carla has found a new friend at the market. It is a nice young boy who feeds her clumps of hay and strokes her neck.
Carla's master and the boy's dad are talking to each other. They seem to get on well with each other, Carla notices. But what are they doing now? Carla is a bit shocked. They are slapping each other's hand. Surely they aren't arguing? Silly Carla. They are shaking hands. That's what people do at the market if they want to buy an animal. Look, the boy's dad has just bought you.
Soon you will go with them and the boy will look after you from now on.

February 28

Little friends

Remus likes it at the children's farm. Even in the winter, the pony does not get bored for one moment because he has so many little friends. Every morning Timmy Bird drops in for a chat. Timmy hops up onto Remus's head to sit on his mane while twittering away. Sometime later, the family of field mice pay a visit and nibble at the straw in Remus's stable.

The little field mice are so bold that they even climb up onto Remus, but he does not mind. Remus likes the attention. Sometimes when Mom and Daddy Field Mouse are busy, Remus looks after the children for them. He lets them swing on his tail. Remus is never bored – he has so many little friends.

March 1

Nina is bored

It has been so cold! There was a frost almost throughout the winter. The entire country was covered in a thick layer of snow. When the snow froze, the ground was slippery and hard. But now the birds are cautiously starting to sing.
"Marie, Marie!" sings the sparrow in the oak tree. "It is spring."
"Peep!" answers the blackbird, Marie, in the chestnut tree.
Sleepily, Nina the pony looks out of the stable window.
When will her master come to fetch her? When will she finally be allowed out? The whole winter she has been kept in the stable. Her master has taken good care of her, of course. But Nina is bored.

March 2

Outdoors

Hey! Here comes Gerry, Nina's master.
He has a halter with him.
"Good morning, Nina!" he calls to her cheerfully.
Nina pricks up her ears.
Did she hear right? Is Gerry more cheerful than usual?
"So, old girl," Gerry says, grabbing her by the mane. "Come here a moment."
Nina needs no second bidding. She happily thrusts her neck into the halter.
"Hey, young'un, not so quick!" laughs Gerry.
Then he opens the stable door.
Nina stands a moment on the threshold before she skips outside.
The spring air tingles her nose.
"Hee-eee!" she snorts. This means that finally spring is coming.

Donkey Droopy Ear

Robin's grandmother has knitted for ever such a long time. But now it is finally ready – Donkey Droopy Ear. Donkey Droopy Ear has been made entirely of scraps of old wool. His body is all the colors of the rainbow. Only the tip of his tail and his mane are black. On top of his head on either side of his mane there are two large, red ears. One stands up straight, one is bent. That's why he is called Donkey Droopy Ear.
"There you are," says Grandma. "I think Robin will be very pleased with you." Then she picks up a sheet of pretty paper that is green with lots of colored dots all over it. She packs Donkey Droopy Ear in the paper for Robin.

March 4

Robin's birthday

Robin got out of bed very early. So early that everyone else is still asleep: Daddy, Mommy and even Jasper the dog. Why does Robin get up so early? It is only just half-past four. Robin cannot sleep. He is too excited. He is also full of curiosity. It is Robin's birthday today.
He is five years old. He wants to know what present he will get.
He just cannot sleep. But everybody else is fast asleep! Even the sun is not yet up. On tiptoes, Robin creeps back to bed. I hope they haven't forgotten, he thinks, staring at the ceiling.

March 5

Hip hip hooray!

About six o'clock Robin falls asleep again. That is why he does not notice Daddy and Mommy quietly entering his room with Jasper.
"Happy birthday!" cry Daddy and Mommy.
Robin is taken aback. But he quickly remembers – it is his birthday.
"Happy birthday, dear Robin! Happy birthday to you," sing Mommy and Daddy and then they give him a big kiss. Then he is given a lovely big parcel. A train – how nice! Robin is very pleased. That afternoon Grandma comes to see him. Do you know what Granny has brought? Robin quickly tears the paper off the present.
"Oh! A horse. Thank you, Grandma!" he screams in delight.
A horse? Donkey Droopy Ear cannot believe his bright red ears.

March 6

I look like a horse

I might look a bit like a horse,
But I'm not of course.
Perhaps you should consider,
That my ears are so much bigger.
With a momentary perusal,
You'll see my legs aren't unusual.
But if you still don't know,
I'll "ee-aw, ee-aw" for you now.
So there, what am I?

Lola

Lola has lived for years at the riding school. That makes her very old. Nobody actually knows her age. Her ears droop and she has gray hairs in her blond mane. The children do not find her a sound horse.
"Who wants to ride Lola," scorns Peter. "Drippy, stupid Lola."
Peter has ridden for four years. He believes he can ride really well.
"I'm sure I have seen you ride Lola," Andrea teases. "About three or four years ago, you were even happy to be allowed to ride Lola."
That's how it is. Even the boys who now scorn her learned to ride on her.
"Dear, loyal Lola." Andrea strokes her, and cuddles her. "Don't take any notice of them. I still think you're the best in the stables."

March 8

Lola is lame

Andrea has saddled Lola, the elderly, loyal riding school horse. Now she leads her to school by the bridle.
"Wait a moment!" Bianca calls out. She is the owner of the riding school.
"I think Lola is lame." Carefully, Andrea lets Lola take a few more steps.
"No, I'm certain. She is limping. She is definitely lame. Take her back to her box." Bianca instructs.
Poor Lola, the vet must be called.
"Lola must rest for three weeks," he announces somberly.
Lola's ears hang down lower than usual. Andrea is determined to visit her every day.
"We'll must get you better quickly," she tells the horse.

Don't be afraid

All the children are a bit nervous before their lessons at the riding school, especially those who do not yet ride very well.

"May I ride Lola?" Lisa asks Bianca, the owner of the school.

"No. Lola is lame. Why don't you ride Charlie," Bianca answers cheerfully. Lisa is puzzled. Oh heavens! She does not dare ride Charlie.

Charlie often misbehaves. He bucks and rears. With a pounding heart, Lisa later enters the school riding Charlie.

The horse sweeps his tail happily and takes a couple of tripping steps.

"Don't be afraid, Lisa," says Bianca.

"Charlie will know if you are frightened."

March 10

A wild buck

Lisa knows perfectly well that you must not be nervous when you ride Charlie. Charlie is a mischievous pony, but he doesn't mean any harm. He is just playful. That's why she tries hard to be brave throughout the lesson.

"Now let's try a gallop," calls Bianca, who is teaching the lesson.

"Remember to push your horse on with your legs and hands. Gallop!"

Charlie understands everything Bianca says. Lisa has no need to do anything. Charlie does it all. He is so happy that he makes a couple of wild bucks.

"Ahhh!" screams Lisa. She is just able to hang on to his mane. Fortunately.

"Well done, Lisa!" calls Bianca.

"You see, there's no need to be scared."

Will Lisa want to ride Charlie for the next lesson?

March 11

Nick wants to ride a horse

Nick wants to ride a horse. It is something he has wanted to do for ages, or at least six months. But however much he whines about it, Mommy and Daddy do not agree.
"You're only four, Nick. We think you're too young. Perhaps in a couple of years," they always say.
Bah, how boring Nick finds that! Do you know why he wants to ride a horse?
Because he wants to be a cowboy and go to live in Montana and have a huge ranch with thousands of cows.
That's why he needs to be able to ride really well – and to lasso with a rope.
"If I'm not allowed to ride a horse, I'll practice with the lasso," says a very angry young Nick.

March 12

Nicky the Kid

There is Nicky the Kid,
Seated on his black horse,
Best cowboy in all the land,
Complete with lasso in hand,
Driving a thousand head of cattle,
Over mountains, yippee I aye,
To his ranch down on the prairie.
Come on, little doggies, come on.

March 13

The best uncle in the world

"Hey, Nicky," calls Mommy. "Guess who is coming to see us? Uncle Tom! Uncle Tom from Montana."

Uncle Tom is Mommy's brother. Nick has met him once.

That afternoon, a red Jeep pulls up outside their house. And yes, it is Uncle Tom. He looks like a cowboy. He has a leather jacket and stout boots.

"Hello, Nicky," says Uncle Tom.

"Look what I have brought you from Montana." Uncle Tom pulls a hobby horse out of a large plastic bag.

"A real cowboy horse," shouts Nick.

His head is of soft, white material and he has a blond mane. And do you know what the nicest part is? If you press his left ear, he whinnies. Press his right ear and he snorts.

Nick thinks Uncle Tom is the best uncle in the world.

March 14

Tom the cowboy horse

Nick has given his hobby horse a fine, sturdy name: Tom – just like his Uncle Tom from Montana. For Uncle Tom brought the hobby horse all the way from Australia. The whole day, Nick gallops around the house with Tom. Cowboy horses are clever and agile. They can go really anywhere: up and down stairs, in the bedroom, the kitchen and even the bathroom. At night, cowboy horse Tom does not sleep in an ordinary stable, like other horses. No, cowboy horse Tom is allowed in bed with his master because he is so special.

"Just as long as he doesn't whinny!" Mommy says.

Ringo and Basil

Ringo is a cheerful Shetland pony and Miranda is
his mistress. Ringo and Miranda are very lucky
because they live on a lovely farm together in the
middle of the wood. Ringo has a fine stable and a
lush, green meadow full of tender, succulent grass
all to himself.
Well, not completely to himself. Because Miranda
also has a delightful patched rabbit called Basil.
Basil is allowed to keep Ringo company in the
meadow. "Otherwise you would spend the whole
day grazing and become too fat," Miranda tells
Ringo.
Ringo enjoys the company of Basil. But he says
that Basil eats too much grass.

March 16

Scared of water

Every day Miranda and Ringo go for a ride
through the wood. That is usually great fun,
except when it has rained. Then there are huge
puddles everywhere on the paths through the
wood. "Walk on, Ringo." Miranda spurs her pony
on. But try as she might, Ringo refuses to go
through the puddle. Ringo is scared of water. Go
through the water yourself, thinks Ringo, you
won't see me doing so.
Miranda always has to dismount.
"Look, Ringo, it's not deep at all."
Carefully, hoof by hoof, Ringo follows
his mistress.

March 17

A horse and a rabbit

A rabbit and a horse
Can be friends, of course.
You might believe it if you saw them
Romping madly without decorum.
Look! Basil and Ringo together
Are both chasing a feather.
They play all day when they are able
And at night they share the stable.

March 18

Prairie Flower and the black foal

Prairie Flower is an Indian princess. She has beautiful, long black plaits and wears moccasins of the finest leather on her feet. Prairie Flower is the favorite of her father, the chief. She is given everything her heart desires. But Prairie Flower is a modest girl. She is quite satisfied and has no unfulfilled wishes. But one day, one of the mares belonging to the chief gives birth to a gorgeous foal. His coat gleams as brightly as Prairie Flower's black plaits.
"Oh, Papa," says the little princess.
"I would love to have that foal." The wise tribal chief smiles. "Dearest Prairie Flower, you know I will give you anything you ask, but a horse can never belong to you. A horse can only be your friend."
From that day, Prairie Flower took good care of the gray foal.
Do you think the foal will be her friend?

60

March 19

My own pony

Chloe is getting her own pony. What a day! This afternoon he will be brought by horse trailer. She has gotten everything ready with Daddy. There is a small stable next to the house with hay in it. There is a sack of oats in the shed and some carrots. And, of course, they have not forgotten all the grooming instruments. Everything looks perfect. Chloe has dreamed of how she will take care of Little Fox. She will feed him and groom him. And take him for a ride every day. Chloe's dream is coming true.

March 20

Mucking out

Little Fox has been with Chloe for a week now and they are both very happy and satisfied. Little Fox gets delicious food and is groomed, made a fuss of and also taken out daily.
Chloe is very happy. There is just one thing wrong. She hates mucking out his stall.
"Will you muck out for me, Daddy?" she asks hopefully.
Daddy laughs. "No, darling!" he replies.
"He is your pony. You have the fun with him.
You must do the boring parts too."
Secretly Chloe knows that Daddy's right.

Spring

It is very early in the morning. Thin wisps of mist hang over the meadow, but the sun's early rays are breaking through.

It promises to be a fine spring day. And on this marvelous day, a foal will be born, right there in the meadow. Edda, the Fjord mare, is as around as a barrel and she knows there is not much longer to wait. First come the foal's forelegs and then his head. Once his head appears, plop comes the rest of the colt, all at once.

Still a little stunned, he lies in the grass.

His mother, Edda, gently licks him clean and gently nudges him with her nose at the same time.

"Up you go, on your legs!" she calls tenderly.

First his bottom sticks up and soon the foal is standing on four very wobbly, long, spindly legs. Amazing, isn't it?

We cannot walk so quickly!

March 22

Clever Edda

"Mommy, Daddy, come quickly – look!" shouts Jeremy. Completely out of breath, he comes running into the kitchen. "Edda…. the meadow…. just happened."
He cannot get his words out.
"Take it easy," laughs Daddy. "What is the matter?"
But Daddy has already realized what it is. "Has the foal arrived?"
Together with Jeremy they run into the garden. There in the meadow is Edda, the proud mother of the young colt.
Unsteadily, he walks behind his mother.
"Oh, how wonderful!" says Mommy, who is still in her bathrobe.
"Yes," agrees Jeremy. "Clever Edda did it all on her own."
"Tell you what, let's leave them in peace," says Daddy. "Then I'll telephone the vet."

March 23

Maternity visit

Edda has a son! Have you heard the news?
Edda has a strong, new son! Like wildfire, the news spreads around the farm.
"We must go to see them soon," says the giant farm horse, Peter.
"Oh, I am so curious!" snorts Birgit, the other Fjord mare. She had a foal herself last year. Her foal is a year old and has no interest in baby foals.
Bertha the cow likes foals.
"Let's all go together," she moos.
A little while later, all the animals from the farm line up along the fence to the meadow: Peter, Birgit, Bertha.
Even the sheep and goat have joined them.
"Congratulations, Edda!" they call to her in unison.

March 24

In the attic

Up in the attic full of junk in a big, old house stands Isabel, the rocking horse. Isabel is still very beautiful, yet she has been banished to the attic. Do you know why? The children to whom Isabel was given have all outgrown her. They are too big for a rocking horse. This makes Isabel very sad. She yearns to play with cheerful children. Don't worry, Isabel! The children think it's a shame you are put away up here. Look, there is Emma. "Yes, here is Isabel," she calls down. Then she picks up Isabel. What is she doing?

March 25

A spring clean

"There, I'm going to give you a good clean," says Emma. Isabel the rocking horse is then treated to a complete spring clean. It is necessary too, for she has been stuck in the dusty attic for four years. But soon she gleams like never before. Even her little red saddle dazzles your eyes.
"Wow! She's so beautiful!" exclaims Emma's mother in surprise a little later.
"I think so too," says Emma. "I think lots of children are going to have fun with Isabel! Shall we go?" With Isabel under her arm, she walks to the car. Where is she taking Isabel?

March 26

A rocking horse at the riding school

Emma takes her lovely, loyal rocking horse to Bianca's riding school. There is a small snack room at the riding school where lots of small children play. "Oh, thank you so much, Emma!" gushes Bianca. Bianca is the owner of the riding school. "Now the little ones can also ride a horse."
Isabel is given a place of honor in the snack room. Lots of children play on her, from early morning until late in the evening. There is Benny, Bianca's little son, and Natasha, the neighbor's daughter, but also Miranda, who always comes with her mother. They take turns riding on Isabel. They are practicing for later. And Isabel? She is the happiest rocking horse in the whole world!

March 27

To the slaughterhouse?

Sheila has been taking care of Bruno, the old horse of Farmer Hagley. Bruno is
twenty-four years old. He can no longer work on the farm, but Sheila takes him
for a short ride every day. She learned to ride on him. Sheila loves Bruno.
But one day, Farmer Hagley says:
"Don't bother to come tomorrow, Sheila."
"Why not?" asks Sheila in surprise.
"Bruno is going away tomorrow," replies the farmer.
"Where to?" asks Sheila. Tears of disappointment well in her eyes.
"To the slaughterhouse," responds the farmer.
To the slaughterhouse? That must not happen, thinks Sheila. But what can she do?

March 28

Retirement

Sobbing, Sheila tells her family what is to become of Bruno.

"Is Farmer Hagley really going to send Bruno to the slaughterhouse?" demands her mother in high indignation.

Sheila's father understands, though.

"I'm afraid that's how it is. An animal that's no longer useful is gotten rid of."

Even so, Dad decides to go to talk to Farmer Hagley.

"That horse won't fetch much," he says.

"Not so," responds the farmer. "The slaughterhouse will give me five hundred dollars for him."

"Hagley, if I give you three hundred dollars, will you let Bruno stay in your field?"

Farmer Hagley scratches his ear.

"All right. Agreed!" he answers.

That's how Bruno went into retirement. He does not must work for Farmer Hagley anymore and Sheila can take of him for years to come.

March 29

The colt show

Pat has been run off her feet! The entire stable must look its best and all the horses must be groomed. Today, after all, is the colt show. People are coming from all over the country to see if they can find a suitable colt for their mare at Pat's stud farm. Pat has beautiful Arabs – Abdullah and Chapoor are the most important. She also has huge, black Friesian horses with long, flowing manes called Melle and Jelle. Pat also has pretty mares with young foals that are the children of Abdullah, Chapoor, Melle and Jelle. Four days ago, another Arab foal was born. He is called Aladdin. Should she put Aladdin on show? Pat is uncertain. Won't he be afraid of all those people?

March 30

Aladdin steals the show

Hundreds of people have come to visit Pat's stud farm because she is holding a colt show today. Pat stands by Fatima's box. Fatima is Aladdin's mother. Fatima looks at her calmly with great, shining eyes.
"What do you think, Fatima?" Pat asks the mare. "Should we let everybody see Aladdin today?" Aladdin playfully whisks his tail.
"It will be all right," decides Pat. Sometime later, she leads Fatima by her halter into the ring.
"Ladies and gentlemen! A gentle but appreciative applause for Fatima and Aladdin, son of Chapoor. He is only four days old." Somewhat surprised, Aladdin trots behind his mother. He looks around him curiously. Everyone is smiling and applauding. What a lovely, handsome little foal he is!

Aladdin the Arab

Aladdin is still quite tiny
And full of zest for life.
But once he is full grown
A proud Arab stallion he'll be.

Everyone will gasp and say,
Oh, what a magnificent beast!
Aladdin quite conceitedly
Will raise his nose and say,
I am Aladdin the Arab,
The handsomest horse of all.

April 1

Knit a horse?

James's grandma knits really well. Every winter, she knits socks for the entire family. James is very proud of Grandma, but her socks itch terribly.
"Granny dear," he asks her. "Can you knit me something other than socks this winter?"
Grandma was taken aback. "Of course, James dear. What would you like me to knit you? A tie or a hat?"
James shakes his head. "No, Granny. Can you knit me a horse – a cuddly toy horse that I can take to bed?"
"Well, that might be difficult." Grandma has never knitted a horse. She must think about it.

April 2

Sock horse

Today is the big day. Grandma called on the telephone to say that she has finished James's cuddly horse. James is trembling with anticipation. He can hardly wait for Grandma to arrive. But when he sees the horse Grandma has made, he is surprised. It is a very strange horse.
The horse's head is a sock, his four legs are all socks and they are all different colors. The body is striped like a zebra. The mane and tail have all the colors of a rainbow. James bursts into laughter.
"What a lovely horse, Granny! Nobody else has such a beautiful sock horse."

April 3

Early riser

Johnny was out of bed early this morning. He has mucked out the stall. Carefully, he put all the clean straw to one side and took out the dirty straw and droppings and piled it on the manure heap. It is hard work. But Johnny knows that if you have your own pony, you must take care of it. Mucking out the stall is a necessary part of keeping a horse.

"Hey! Finished at last!" Satisfied with a job done well, he goes home. Mother is making sandwiches. Thank goodness! Johnny's tummy is rumbling after all that hard work.

"Hi, Mom!" he calls. "Is breakfast ready? I'm as hungry as a horse!"

April 4

Hunger

"I think you could eat as much as that pony of yours, Johnny," his mother says. "What did you give him? You left the pony treats behind!"

Johnny looks crestfallen.

"Oh, poor Timmy! I forgot to give him any breakfast."

Johnny runs out of the kitchen and grabs the bag of pony treats, which he should have taken to the stables. It is quite heavy, but he almost runs all the way to the stable.

"How could I have forgotten Timmy!" he rebukes himself.

It might have saved Johnny time if he had remembered before he dashed home for his breakfast because there are already oats and hay at the stable. The pony treats are just for added protein.

"That'll teach me a lesson. I'll be more careful."

April 5

Sorry

"Sorry, Timmy! How could I forget your breakfast?"
Johnny makes a special fuss over his pony, who is surprised, but pleased to see him. "I thought I wasn't going to get anything to eat," mumbles Timmy, snorting into Johnny's hand as it strokes his muzzle.
"Tomorrow I'll bring you carrots and sugar lumps," Johnny promises.

April 6

Breakfast

Johnny's mother is busy in the kitchen. Johnny is always so hungry when he has been working in the stable in the morning. He has to get up early and eat breakfast before he goes. Today she cooks him a second egg, an extra helping of bacon, more fried bread, two sausages, mushrooms and tomatoes.
When Johnny has eaten all of this, he looks at his mother.
"Are you still hungry, Johnny?"
"As hungry as a horse, Mom."
She butters him some bread and spreads his favorite jam on it.
"Then you'll need some high energy food, like those pony treats."
"Thanks, Mom!" he says with a huge smile as he sees what she has cooked and put on his plate.

73

April 7

Manus

Manus is a very old horse. Chump, chump, chump, he chews his way through the meadow. He is happy with his life. The whole day is spent out of doors in the fresh air. He has as much grass as he needs. If Manus could sing, he would probably do so. Every day he sees other horses pass by in the lane alongside his field. Sometimes they have a rider on their back, other times they are pulling a cart or trap.
"Bah!" Manus snorts through his teeth. "I'm glad I don't have to do *that* anymore."

April 8

Shetland

"Ha ha, tee-hee," the other children at the riding school laugh. They point to Gemma. Gemma has come to the riding lesson today on her own pony. Her pony is a Shetland, a barrel on short, little legs.
"You won't be laughing when you see how my Shetland performs in the lesson!" Gemma assures them. And Gemma is right. When the ponies are asked to trot and gallop, Gemma's Shetland goes into top gear. He flies past all the others on his short, little legs.
After the lessons, the children all make a fuss over Gemma's pony. "Gosh, you are fast," they say. "You're just like a little racehorse."

Bucking mood

Every afternoon after school, Martina visits the pony she takes care of. She is friendly and usually does precisely what Martina tells her to. But not today! Petra the pony keeps shying away when Martina tries to saddle her. Eventually, she manages to get the saddle on her. She then mounts the pony.
"Petra! What's up with you today?" grumbles Martina. The pony wants to go the wrong way. Martina gets impatient with her. She grabs her whip to teach her a lesson.
"You've another thought coming," whinnies Petra as she makes a vigorous buck. Martina makes an arched flight to the ground.
"I reckon Petra is in a bucking mood today!" sighs Martina.

April 10

Bareback

"Today I am going to ride bareback," declares Freddie with determination.
"Just like the Indians."
Freddie walks to the field where his horse is kept. He wants to leap up onto his horse's back like a real Indian. He grabs her mane and leaps.
"Gosh! It's a long way up!" he screeches.
Freddie tries again and again, but he can't do it.
He cannot leap high enough.
"I'll never be a true Indian," he sighs sadly.
Then he notices a feather lying on the ground. He sticks it in his hair. At least he can look like an Indian. But can he climb up onto his pony still wearing the feather?

April 11

Clever animals

Carla is in hot water. Dad and Mom are very annoyed with her. Do you know why? Carla did not close the gate to the meadow properly. All five of her father's horses got out. They were only rounded up and put back in the field after a lot of trouble.
"Don't let it happen ever again," grumbles her father. He looks out of the window angrily. What! There are several mischievous horse heads outside the window. Dad cannot understand. He shut the gate himself this time just to make sure. "Did those clever animals open the gate themselves?"

April 12

Muzzle

A horse's great enormous mouth
Is filled with huge, yellow teeth.
And the soft lips of his muzzle
He may use like a pair of hands.
So that with lots of patience,
He might even open gates
And take himself off far away,
Before you catch him.

April 13

Miller's horse

"Hey, look at the enormous hindquarters on that horse!" exclaims Bianca.

"Yes." Grandma nods in agreement. "I reckon that's a real miller's horse."

"What does a miller need with such a horse, Gran?"

"I don't mean a windmill or a watermill, Bianca," explains Grandma. "Where it was not suitable for either, people still needed grain to be ground. They didn't have shops selling flour in those days. A really big horse like that was useful to harness to a pole attached to a millstone. The horse walked around and around in circles, milling the grain."

"How sad," Bianca considered. "The poor horse would get dizzy from going around in circles."

April 14

A donkey?

Giles is a strange animal. He isn't a horse. His ears are much too long. But he is also not a donkey. Donkeys are smaller and have a tail with a brush at its tip.

Giles is a mule. His father was a donkey, but his mother was a horse. Quite satisfied with himself, Giles considers his gray coat.

"I might be a bit strange," he says, "But I have lots of relations. Not just horse aunts and uncles, but donkey nephews and nieces."

April 15

Shock

"Tom, Tom, come quickly," calls Mrs. Simonds. Tom is in bed. He does not understand. But he jumps out of bed even though it is still dark outside. Sleepy-eyed, he stumbles downstairs.
"What's up, Mom?" he demands.
Mom is very mysterious. "Just go to the stable – you'll see."
With his jacket over his pajamas, Tom pulls on his boots. There is a light in the stable and voices. Tom sees his father and the vet.
"Is Nicky sick?" he asks fearfully.
"No, no, Tom," his father says soothingly.
"Something wonderful has happened."

April 16

Congratulations

Nicky is down in the straw. The pony is panting and blowing and also sweating.
"Hi, Nicky!" Tom calls to her. "Come here, girl."
Normally the pony comes to him immediately he calls her. Now she just pricks her ears and whinnies softly.
Then Tom notices that there is something in the straw beside Nicky. It has four long, spindly legs and a short tail.
"Oh! She's had a foal!" Tom cries out. He is so happy that tears pour from his eyes. He is so proud of Nicky. "Well done, Nicky! Congratulations," he adds softly.

April 17

Rain

It has rained all day. Only when school was let out that afternoon did the sun appear. That was fortunate; otherwise all the children would get wet biking home.

Annette has worked so hard at school that she has not noticed the rain. At home she goes straight to her pony. The sun is shining and she is in such a hurry that she decides to ride bareback. She jumps up onto her pony's soaking wet back.

"Yuck!" Now she is soaked through. Silly girl!

April 18

A lovely roll

Mickey is a rascal. His two jet black horse eyes look at the world mischievously. Mickey is crazy about his mistress. She brushes his strawberry roan coat so beautifully. Grooming never lasts long enough for him.

"There, you look lovely once more," his mistress tells him at the end of an hour's work with dandy brush and body brush. "Now you can go out into the field."

But Mickey stills itches everywhere, especially on his back. As soon as he is in the meadow, he rolls on his back.

"Oh, Mickey!" shouts his mistress. "Now you're filthy again. You're covered in green and brown patches once more. I'm not grooming you again!"

Blacksmith

There is excitement in the stables. The horses have heard that the blacksmith is coming today. Two pretty mares can talk of nothing else.
"I hope it's my turn today. I need new shoes," says the first.
"Me too," says the second mare. "I hope he has some smart new shoes with him. Those nice, shining ones look so nice."
"Bah!" snorts a colt, in another stall a little further along.
"I can't stand all that hammering on my hooves. When it's my turn, you're welcome to take my place."

April 20

Clip, clop

Clip, clop, clip, clop!
rings out up and down the street.
Most people are quite happy,
listening to the sound of horses' feet.

Clip, clop, clip, clop!
click the horse's hooves.
Clip, clop, clip, clop!
echoing from walls and roofs.

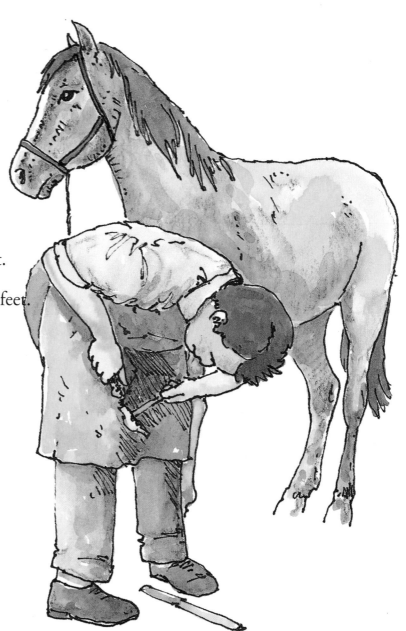

April 21

Arabella

Arabella is a very strange horse. She is unbelievably pretty with pink and blue piebald markings. Her lustrous mane is so long it almost touches the ground. On top of that, Arabella is such an easy horse. She never needs grooming. One wipe over with a cloth is sufficient to keep her clean. And she does not eat oats and hay.

"No," says Arabella, "I've no desire for hay or grass. Yet I can still move." What a strange horse! Arabella is a toy horse made of plastic. All she needs is a replacement battery now and then. Then she can take slow paces and whinny.

April 22

Wind

"I am clever," neighs Bonny the pony. It is raining cats and dogs. The other ponies stand close together to keep as dry as possible. But Bonny is standing under a group of trees for protection. Beneath their branches, she keeps quite dry. She waits until the shower has passed by.

"You are all really soaked!" she laughs at the others. When the sun shines again, the other ponies shake the water off themselves. The wind will do the rest. But the wind does something else as well. It is blowing through the trees and it blows all the raindrops off the trees onto Bonny. Poor Bonny, you are not as clever as you thought you were.

April 23

Knights

Knights are very bold
And do such daring deeds
But where do you think a knight
would be without his trusty steed?
His armor and equipment
Are far too heavy, yes indeed,
For a knight to fight on foot,
However tough the breed.
But seated high upon a horse
He rides forth to meet his fate,
But never mind his mount, of course,
Who has to bear his weight.

April 24

Pluto

Pluto is a true knight's steed. He has fought hard and taken part in many tournaments. Pluto is extremely brave. He is not afraid of danger.
"Look at my right-hand hindquarter," says Pluto. "There you can see the scars from my recent battle."
Yet Pluto still sighs when they take him out of his stable. Fighting is not a problem for him, but carrying that heavy knight upon his back is.
"Consider how much such a knight weighs," Pluto says. "He is covered from top to bottom in armor. Together the knight and his armor weigh more than two hundred pounds. No, I'd be happy to fight if I didn't have an iron can on my back."

April 25

Rumpety, tumpety, tumpety, tum

Hooray! Grampy is coming. It is always such fun when Grampy comes to visit. Grampy knows super games to play, games from very long ago. Some of them are peaceful games like "I spy with my little eye." But the best games of all are the rambunctious ones, reckons Dick. Specially the one where Granddad sits him on his knee and bounces him, singing, "Rumpety, tumpety, tumpety, tum." He bounces up and down on Grampy's knees. Dick knows the song by heart. He knows what happens at the end of it. That's when Grampy lets him fall between his knees. Dick howls with delight because he knows Grampy will always catch him.

April 26

Pony tail

Little Janet is very lazy. She is also very pretty. She has beautiful, dark eyes and long, blond hair. It comes almost down to her shoulders. Yet it is not long enough for Janet.
"I want a real pony tail!" she repeats all the time. Every morning, her mother fixes her blond hair with a hair band. But Janet is not satisfied. One day she secretively steals away to the meadow with a pair of scissors. Just as she is about to cut off one of the pony's tails, her mother comes running.
"Don't be so naughty! If you really want a pony tail, you must have some patience. Perhaps it would help if you acted like a pony. After all, you can already whinny!"

Milkman

Twice a week the milkman comes to the farm. He brings all kinds of groceries and items for the farmer's wife in his van.
"Beep beep!" toots his horn as he comes up the drive. Tiffany the pony no longer jumps when the milkman toots his horn. Instead, she runs over to him. She waits until the milkman opens the doors of his vehicle.
"What has he got on board?" Tiffany wants to know. She sticks her muzzle inside the van. "Mmm, that smells nice!"
Unfortunately, the milkman does not want ponies in his vehicle.
"Get out, old girl!"

April 28

Lazybones

Most horses do not sleep a great deal. While the dew is still fresh on the ground, they are usually awake. Not Chester though. Chester is a lazybones. He is happiest snoozing in the straw.
"Hoo-aaah!" yawns Chester, exposing his yellow teeth. "The mornings are so busy here on the farm. The milkman clangs the milk bottles, the pigs snort, the cows moo. A respectable horse can hardly catch forty winks!"
Despite this, Chester is good friends with the other animals on the farm. Only one creature is the object of hatred – Cyril the rooster.
"That wretched crowing cock-a-doodle-doo wakes me up every morning. I have an overwhelming desire to fill his beak full of hay."

April 29

Bugs

A new foal has been born. It is a lovely colt with very long legs.
"How sweet," thinks Anne. "Look what a cute little tail he has. It is just like a bit of brown fluff."
"Yes." Ingrid, her sister, nods. "Look at those ears. Aren't they long!" This makes Anne laugh.
"With that tail and those ears, he looks more like a rabbit than a foal. Tell you what, we'll call him Bugs Bunny. Just like in the cartoons."
Ingrid agrees it's a good idea. "I hope he is as clever as Bugs."

April 30

Mother

Mom Mare takes good care
Says to her foal: "Now, you beware
That always by my side you stay
And don't ever, ever, run away.
Stay where I can always see you
Here where I can safely guard you.
It's not that I wish to chide,
But let me always be your guide."

May 1

Fright

Tinker the pony is in the meadow. He has discovered a couple piles of earth.
How funny! They were not there yesterday. Curiosity gets the better of him and
he sniffs at the heaps.
"Hey! What was that?" One of the heaps has gotten bigger. Scrabble, scrabble,
little bits of soil fall out of the center of the heap. Angrily, Mister Mole sticks his
head out.
"Do you mind leaving my home alone, you great beast!"
Tinker had not expected this. He jumps back on all four legs in fright and
gallops off.
"There you are," says Mr. Mole. "That got rid of him."

May 2

Large and small

It has often times been said
Being small need hold no dread.
The giant horse is scared to bits
By a tiny mole who has got his wits.
Thinks Mole, I've never ridden any nag,
He don't frighten me, that's no brag.
But he's sure terrified of me,
Look at the way I made him flee
By putting on an angry voice.
Small, but brave, is the best choice.

Mug

The vet comes to look at the horses. Before he leaves, he gives Ronald's mother a jar of ointment.
"Rub this into their legs and that will deal with your problem," says the vet. "That should clear things up within a week."
Ronald has been listening and while Mom says good-bye to the vet, he takes the ointment and takes all the mugs off the shelf and starts to smear them with the ointment. Mom returns.
"Ronald! Stop that! What are you doing?"
"The vet said you had to make sure all the mugs were smeared with this ointment."
"No, no, sweetie! Two of the horses have rain rot. The vet says we must smear the areas on their legs with the ointment – not mug, my darling."
"Now I understand," says Ronald.
"I thought it was strange."

May 4

The cheese merchant

The cheese merchant is worried. Every day except Sunday, he takes his cheese to sell at the market. But business is not good.
"It seems that children don't like cheese anymore," he sighs. "And cheese is so good for them."
He scratches behind his ear. "If I don't sell more soon, I won't have enough money to feed my horse. Then I will must sell her."
That would be a pity, for the cheese merchant is very fond of his horse, Madeleine.
But perhaps there is a solution for the cheese merchant.

Old-fashioned

It is very busy at the market. All the mothers and fathers are doing their shopping. There are long lines at the fruit and vegetable booth and also at the fishmonger. But busiest of all is the cheese merchant. All the children want to go to the cheese booth today. They drag their parents with them.

"Are you going to buy some cheese, Mommy?" and "We need more cheese, Dad!" Do you know what – the cheese man has swapped his modern van for an old-fashioned horse-drawn wagon.

The children all want to see the cheese man's horse. The cheese merchant's face beams. He has sold more cheese today than he sold all last week.

"Tasty cheese, fresh eggs!" he calls out.

"Old-fashioned quality!"

Anthony and Antonia

Anthony and Antonia are a wonderful couple. They pull a cart through the woods and along the beach almost every day. Many tourists want to ride in their cart. Some are nice people, but some scream and shout a lot. When the horses realize that they have noisy people on board, they play a trick on them.

The walk calmly until they come to a steep section of track. Then with a wink of the eye from Anthony to Antonia, they make a sudden move toward a deep rut in the track.

The people scream as the cart bumps. They are scared stiff but they become very quiet.

"Now we can get some peace," sighs Antonia contentedly.

May 7

Cock of the walk

Most of the horses in the field are very calm. The mares all take good care of their foals. The foals all do what their mothers tell them. Except Viking, that is. Viking is a mischievous colt foal. He is a wild monkey and extremely curious to boot. He is always the first on the scene. When they are fed, Viking is already there at the trough. And if something happens right at the other end of the field, Viking almost trips over himself in his efforts to get there as quickly as possible. "What a shame," sighs his mother. "That foal is misnamed. They should have called him King of the Hill."

May 8

Prick

Viking, the young foal, is alert. There is a car coming this way. Viking is there by the field gate when the man gets out of his car.
"So then, boy," says the man. "Not scared, I see."
Viking does not realize that the man is the vet. Today he has come to inoculate the horses against the flu. Viking has never had an injection. He thinks that the man has come to do something nice. What a surprise he gets when the man suddenly pricks him. He whinnies and gallops quickly to his mother.
"That will teach you not to be King of the Hill," his mother says without sympathy.

Thunder

Mr. Lightning is a photographer. He is famous because he takes the very best pictures of horses. Today he is to take photographs of Thunder. Thunder is a true champion. He is a wonderful colt and has already won major competitions. Driving to the shoot, Mr. Lightning laughs.
"It wouldn't surprise me at all," he says, "if Thunder and Lightning together didn't cause something of a storm."

May 10

Rascal

The storm brewing is Mr. Lightning's temper. Every time he gets Thunder lined up to photograph him, the colt moves just as he is about to press the shutter. Thunder just will not stand still. Mr. Lightning has tried all the soothing words he knows. But he is angry now because he is sure that Thunder is doing it on purpose. The horse walks away every time he is ready to take a photograph.
Mr. Lightning is feeling thunderous.

Tabitha

Tabitha the cat comes to see what is going on. She sees a man standing in the field with a strange piece of equipment. Tabitha is a bit concerned. "What is he doing to my friend, Thunder?" she meows. Tabitha is best friends with Thunder. When the cats walks into the field, Thunder suddenly becomes very calm. Tabitha walks up to him very carefully, then does a couple of little leaps. The man in the meadow suddenly looks very happy. He puts his camera up to his face. Click, click, click, hears Tabitha.
She does not know that the man is a photographer and that she is being very helpful to him. Finally he can take his photographs.

May 12

Thanks

Mr. Lightning is finished. He has shot several rolls of film and he is very happy. "These are the best horse photographs I've ever taken," he sighs with pleasure. "I should thank that cat. Without her, I'd never have got that horse calm." Mr. Lightning walks to the farm and asks for a saucer of milk. "Here, pussy," he says. "Thanks for your help." Tabitha doesn't understand any of it. She always goes to Thunder in his field every day. This is the first time anyone has given her milk for doing so.

Esmeralda

A gypsy caravan is being pulled along a country lane. It is the home of Conchita the fortune teller. Conchita is visiting the farms to tell people what the future has in store for them. She earns a little money to feed herself and her horse, Esmerelda. Conchita takes good care of Esmerelda because she pulls the caravan. Esmerelda also knows a few tricks. If Conchita holds out an apple, Esmerelda will hold out a hoof. And if Conchita asks Esmerelda how many two plus two make, the horse whinnies four times. The people sometimes give Conchita more money for Esmerelda's tricks than they pay for the fortune telling.

May 14

Luck

George has found a horseshoe. He knows that horseshoes only bring you luck if you hang them on a wall. George immediately looks for a hammer and nail.
Bang, bang, bang.
The next-door neighbor passes by. "George, you've done it wrong. If the gap is at the bottom, all the luck will run out."
"Oh dear!" says George. That will never do, he thinks. Quickly he fastens it to the wall the other way up.
"Now you must hope that plenty of luck will fall into it," laughs his neighbor.

May 15

Putting on weight

Anthony and Antonia are pulling a cart. They work well together as a team and they also love each other. They make an attractive pair between the shafts. Except not today.

"Stop pushing!" grumbles Anthony.

"I'm not!" snarls Antonia. "You are pushing me."

"You've been eating too much, " complains Anthony. "You're putting on weight. Your belly is getting too fat to go between the shafts."

This starts a real quarrel between them. The silly horses don't realize that Antonia isn't getting fat from eating too much. She is pregnant. That's why she is growing so large. Fortunately their master knows. He decides that Antonia should remain in the meadow until her foal is born.

May 16

Mum and Dad

Anthony and Antonia
The stallion and the mare,
Love each other very much,
They're a truly devoted pair.
Anthony's to be a father soon
A foal for dear Antonia, they say.
No longer will they be just two.
A new colt or filly's due any day.

Dandelions

Farmer Wilson's field is full of yellow dandelions. The entire field is bright yellow. There is not a blade of green grass to be seen. Here comes the farmer. He is coming to look at Turk, his gray. "Well, I'll be!" exclaims the farmer. "Where's that horse got to?" He peers and peers, but cannot see anything. But wait – something moved. It is Turk. Turk is as yellow as the dandelions that surround him. He has rolled in them and is covered in yellow pollen. When Farmer Wilson slaps his back, a great yellow cloud covers him.

May 18

Sea horse

Saxon the pony is very hot. The sun is very strong and Saxon cannot find any shade to protect him.

"Perhaps a drink of water will help," he whinnies. The pony walks to a ditch at the edge of his field. It has been dry for so long that there is very little water in the ditch. Saxon has to bend his head really low to reach the water. Still he has to stretch further.... splash! Now Saxon is right in the ditch. Mmmm, at least it's cool. Saxon flounders and splashes.

"Hey! Watch it!" croaks a frog. "What do you think you are? A sea horse?"

May 19

Wedding

"It is far too hot to walk, let alone trot," grumbles Crispen. Yet he has to work. Crispen is a carriage horse and the carriage is waiting for him. Today he draws the carriage erratically and with ill humor. Then he sees who the carriage is to carry today.

A beautiful girl in a stunningly lovely white dress emerges from the house where the coachman has drawn him up.

"A bride," whinnies Crispen. "Isn't she lovely! Yippee!" His bad mood is forgotten because he adores brides and weddings. Crispen knows all the guests will spoil him.

May 20

Trailer

Bobby the pony has been sold. Today he will be collected. His new master has just turned up with the trailer. Bobby has to go in the trailer because his new master lives too far away to be led there.

"He-uh-uh," snorts Bobby, frightened of the trailer. He finds it quite nasty. If they think they are going to get him in that, they can think again. Not for a hundred carrots.

A few feet from the trailer, he digs in his hooves and refuses to move. Bobby will not take another step.

May 21

No harm in trying

"Why won't Bobby go in the trailer?" young Jack wonders. His father says: "Bobby doesn't understand. He has never been in a trailer. And since he doesn't understand human language, we cannot explain to him that he has nothing to be afraid of."

Jack is not so sure. He knows that Bobby is a very intelligent pony who understands what you say to him.

"Let me try to calm him down, Dad," Jack suggests. His father looks a bit doubtful.

"How are you going to do that? Oh well, there's no harm in trying."

May 22

Secret

Young Jack walks quietly over to Bobby. He strokes him along his back and on his mane. Bobby likes that. It seems as though he has forgotten about the trailer for a moment. Then Jack stands on tiptoes and whispers into Bobby's ear. No one else can hear what he says. Dad Jack and Bobby's new master cannot believe their eyes as Bobby walks calmly into the trailer.

"How did you get him to do that, Jack?" asks his astounded father.

"Yes, I'd like to know how," added Bobby's new owner.

But Jack will not say. He smiles and says: "That's a secret between Bobby and me."

May 23

King

King lives up to his regal name. He is also a very strong, very calm and sensible horse. This is very important. King is a police horse. He carries a policeman on his back. They make sure together that everything stays calm in the town and on the streets. Before he started work, however, King had to go to school. Not an ordinary school, but a special one for police horses. There the horses must learn to get used to smoke and the sound of shooting, music, screaming people and much more. King was the best horse in his class. Now when he trots through the streets, he is not frightened by backfiring car exhausts. He merely snorts: "That guy needs to take his car to a garage."

May 24

Vacation

Police horses must work hard the whole year. But like people, they enjoy a vacation now and then. Then they are taken to a delightful, quiet place where there are woods, or perhaps near a beach. The horses love their freedom and tranquillity.

"He-ee-ee! This is better than smelly exhaust all around you," whinnies King. His friend Jumper nods in agreement. "I'd a thousand times rather listen to the birds sing than hear the noise of the city."

But after a week of vacation, they are both jittery. Vacation is nice, but they miss their work. They are nicely rested and healthy. Both cannot wait to get back to the city streets.

Old folks home

There is an old folks home on the edge of town. But it is not for elderly people. No, only very old horses live there. The horses have worked hard for people all their lives. In return, they can now rest in this sanctuary for old retired horses. A card by each box gives their details: their name, age and what type of work they did. The horses could tell much more. Unfortunately, people do not understand the language of horses. So we'll never know what Carl, the old street organ horse, is saying to Prince, the farm horse. Or maybe we shall?

Carl

"Mmmm, it is comfortable here in this old folks home," sighs Carl. "Yet don't you miss something?"

"Such as?" whinnies a surprised Prince.

"I miss the music," explains Carl. Carl used to pull an organ through the streets. "The children used to love the sound of the street organ," he adds. "Most of them used to dance when they heard the music. "Ta-ra-ra-boom-di-ay, ta-ra-ra-boom-di-ay." Carl sways gently to and fro in his stall as he remembers the organ playing. "Fortunately, I've heard the tunes so often that I can remember them. Ta-ra-ra-boom-di-ay," muses Carl.

May 27

Ol' bones

Prince, the old farm horse, shakes his head. He is very happy that he does not work anymore. He is not upset that his former owner now uses a tractor.
"Don't you miss the farm at all?" his neighbor Carl inquires.
"Not on your life!" whinnies Prince. "Day in, day out it was hard work pullin' that there plow. Nope! I don't care if I never see a plow again or cart." Prince remembers working on the land and how he and the farmer would make a dead straight furrow across the field.
"My old bones ache when I just think about it." Prince smiles.

May 28

Meek horses

There are more satisfied horses in the sanctuary. Samantha the mare is an old riding school horse. She spent her whole life going around in circles in the riding school. "You're dead right, Prince," she whinnies to the old farm horse. "I never want to work again. You do your best and what do you get? A flick of the whip if you make a mistake."
There are no whips to be found in the horses' sanctuary. That is not necessary. The horses are all so old that any wildness has long since disappeared. They walk around meekly when they are allowed out into the field on a sunny day. They are happy to return to their warm stable in the evening.

Egg

Bonny the pony has a little friend. It is Carla the sparrow. Every day, Carla flutters into the meadow and lands on Bonny's back. But Carla is in a hurry today. She stays for hardly a second or two before she must be off. "Aren't you hungry today?" asks Bonny, somewhat surprised. "Yes and no!" cheeps Carla. "But I'm in a hurry. I must lay an egg. The month is nearly over so I must be quick."

May 30

Eyes shut

Bonny is taken aback by her little friend. The sparrow wants to lay an egg. "Lay an egg? How do you do that?" the pony wants to know. "You choose a good nest. Then you close your eyes and press really hard. The egg just pops out," explains the little bird. "I must try that!" exclaims Bonny. The pony walks to the corner of the field. She closes her eyes and presses really hard. "Yes! Yes! It's working," she cries out. "Something's coming." And when Bonny looks around, she sees a little pile of brown eggs on the grass. So, are they really eggs?

May 31

Misguided

Spring has sprung,
Summer beckons.
The birds are rearing chicks.
But silly pony Bonny
Thinks she has laid eggs
She surely is misguided,
Someone ought to tell her
Those eggs smell dreadful.

105

June 1

Dentist

Billy and his friend Charlie are looking at the field. Three horses are grazing. They have noticed the two boys. They approach the fence curiously where the boys are standing.

The boys stroke the horses' heads. Mmm, that's nice. One of the horses yawns. "Hey! What huge teeth!" cries out Billy.

"But they're so yellow," adds Charlie. "That horse needs to visit the dentist."

"Never! You can't get a horse to a dentist," argues Billy. "Just imagine – a huge thing like that in the dentist's chair with a bib on it." Charlie gets a fit of giggles. Billy always imagines such funny things. The horses do not understand. They know nothing about human dentists. When they have a toothache, the vet comes to them in their field or stable.

Confetti

Martina's new foal does not yet have a name. He has only just been born. He is a very unusual foal. His gray coat is covered with black dots.
"It looks like he has rolled in confetti," she laughs when she sees the foal.
"Yes," agrees Dad. "What do you think of Confetti for a name?"
Martina has to think about it first. She had some much more masculine names in mind for a colt. But Confetti is so suitable.
"Confetti," she says softly. She was sure the foal pricked his ears up. It looks like he wants to answer to that name.

Shower

The horses at the riding school are puffing in the heat. It is very warm today, at least eighty degrees. They loyally do their best at the lesson. The horses know that after the class they will be able to cool off under a shower. They are sprayed with water from a hose. The water is refreshingly cool and they are completely hosed down. It is not just the horses who are suffering from the heat. The riders have red cheeks and look unpleasantly hot. One of the mares has an idea. I will cool my rider off, she thinks. She shakes herself and sprays water all over her rider.
"Great!" The rider laughs. "I need a shower too to cool off."

June 4

Flies

Priscilla the pony likes the fine weather. It is almost summer and the sun is shining. But oh, those flies! They irritate her back and swarm around her legs. She swishes her tail about to try to ward them off. Fortunately, Priscilla has a lovely long tail. Yet still the flies pester her. Flap, flap swings her tail.
"Help, help," buzz the flies. "Let's get out of here.
That flyswatter is far too long."

June 5

Flyswatter

There is no horse
However brave he is
That likes the work of clippers
On his luxuriant growth.
Long hair for horse or pony
Is more than decoration.
It keeps him warm in winter
And now that summer's here,
By swishing it here and there
He holds the flies at bay.
The longest flyswatter of them all –
Especially when used in pairs.

June 6

Line up

Tim and Jeff are friends. Tim is crazy about cars and Jeff is crazy about horses. That's why one day they play with Tim's cars and with Jeff's toy horses the next. Sometimes they play with both together.
"Look at my big truck," says Tim proudly.
"My Shire horse goes with that," suggests Jeff.
Together they work out which vehicle fits with each horse. They line them all up. The Shire horse next to the big truck and the racehorse beside the racing car. At the end of the line, Tim places his Mini. Jeff puts his smallest pony beside it.

June 7

Henry Rabbit

Henry Rabbit is very sad. He is lost. He has gone so far from home that he cannot remember where his burrow is. Worse still, he cannot even see the wood anymore. He is standing in the middle of a field. He begins to cry.
"What's up?" He hears a voice. Henry looks up to see a pretty little pony.
"I'm lost and very tired," he explains.
"Bet you live in the wood," suggests Billy the pony.
"Climb up on my back – I'll take you part of the way home."
If you see a pony with a rabbit on its back, you know it is Billy and Henry.

Human's world

When you are still a young foal, there is much to learn. You must adapt to the human world. That world is full of nasty things.
"He-ee-ee!" whinnies young Jake. "I don't want to live in the human world. I don't like the idea of saddles and bridles – and I absolutely detest screaming children."
His mother shakes her head. "In the world of nature, it is also not so wonderful. You must find your food, even in the winter. In nature, there is no warm stable. You can also forget pony treats and being regularly groomed."
Jake is thoughtful because he had not considered any of these points.

June 9

Shaggy coat

Rasputin is a shaggy pony. He has a very dark coat and a very long unruly mane. He shares his field with some sheep. Provided they leave his fodder alone, Rasputin quite likes the sheep. He often imitates them to amuse himself. But today a strange man has come into the field. He hauls the sheep out one at a time. Rasputin hears the sound of a machine. Curiosity aroused, he investigates and to his horror, he discovers that the man is shearing all the wool off the sheep.
"Oh dear! Maybe I'll be next," he frets. Rasputin does not want to lose his mane. Just to be sure, he hides away in the farthest corner of the field. Don't be silly, Rasputin, you don't have to have your shaggy coat clipped.

Jumper

Jumper is a brown foal that can still fully enjoy his freedom. He dashes about the meadow. But most fun of all is jumping over everything he can find, starting with a pole he found in the field. He clears it with a lovely arc.
Then he leaps over his friend, Beauty, who is sleeping.
"That's going to be a first-class jumper," says his owner excitedly.
He is very happy with Jumper because a good show-jumping horse is worth lots of money.

June 11

Champion jumper

A jumping horse is great to have, but there is a disadvantage. It can jump almost anything, including the gate. That's why Jumper's owner has a plan. He sets up some barrels with poles in the field.
"There you are, jumper. You've no reason to get bored now. See if you can jump these."
Immediately the colt springs over the first jump and then the next.
"He-ee-ee! This is fun!" he whinnies.
"If I practice hard, I might become a champion show jumper."

June 12

Fruit

At the preschool, Teacher is telling the class how healthy fruit is for children. She then asks the children which fruits they like to eat. Many of the children name apples, bananas and oranges, but some children seem never to have eaten any fruit.

"Is there anyone who has never eaten an apple?"

Sarah sticks her hand up.

"Why don't you like apples, Sarah?"

"Oh, I don't hate apples, Teacher. They're the best fruit of all."

Teacher is puzzled. "So why don't you eat them, Sarah? And why do you think they're the best fruit?"

"My pony, Cindy, loves apples. She likes them so much I always give my apple to her, Teacher."

June 13

The Shetland Pony Club

Karen and Rebecca are ever so slightly angry. Rebecca's brother Peter always pokes fun at them because the two girls are crazy about Shetland ponies. You know, those very small ponies.

"Looks like a brush on legs," squeals Peter yet again.

The girls have decided to do something about it. They are setting up a club. A club for everyone who likes Shetland ponies.

Very soon the girls have lots of new friends. They exchange stickers and even have their own magazine, *The Shetland Pony Club Review*. It is such a fun club that Peter wishes he had not been so nasty.

June 14

Not well

Things are dreadful. The farmer is not well. Coughing and protesting, he has been stuck in bed for a week. Patch the dog, Tabitha the cat and Dobbin the horse are worried about him. What can they do? He tries to get out of bed. First one leg…then the other…but he is too weak. He falls back into bed.
"How sad," meows Tabitha.
Patch barks: "He wants to plow the field, but he is too ill."
Dobbin rakes the ground with his hoof.
"Can't we do something to help?"

June 15

Buckles and straps

Dobbin has an idea.
"Surely we could plow the field without the farmer," he suggests to Patch and Tabitha.
"Mmmm," considers Patch, "we can always try."
Together with Tabitha, they go to the old barn. There is the plow.
With his strong teeth, Dobbin pulls it out for the others.
That was the easiest bit. Tabitha jumps up on his back. Together with Patch, they fasten the harness of buckles and straps.
Finally everything is fastened.
"Those buckles were difficult," grumbles Patch.
"Come on, let's go to the field," whinnies Dobbin.

June 16

Teamwork

One can do this, the other that.
A horse is stronger than a cat,
But for work that requires finesse
Not the horse, but the cat has prowess.
And when there's need of good advice,
The dog supplies it in a trice.
When together as a team we work,
There's no task we need to shirk.

June 17

Miracle

The farmer is feeling a little better. He wipes his eyes and looks out of the window. What on earth does he see? His jaw drops in astonishment.
"Well, I'll be darned," he mutters in disbelief. "That's not possible."
What has the farmer seen? Dobbin the horse is plowing the field. Tabitha is seated on his back to make sure he is keeping to a straight line and Patch the dog is holding the plow steady.
"I must be delirious from the fever," he assures himself. "Animals plowing fields! That can't be true. That would be a miracle!"

115

June 18

Pajamas

Nick is at the zoo with Grandma and Granddad. There is lots to see: lions, tigers, elephants and giraffes. Nick skips from the one to the other. Suddenly he tugs at Granddad's jacket.
"Hey, Grampy, what's the time?"
"Eleven o'clock," Granddad replies, somewhat puzzled. "Why do you want to know? Do you want to go home?"
"No." Nick shakes his head. "But those horses have still got their pajamas on and it's eleven o'clock." Granddad laughs loudly. "Silly boy! Those are zebras. They always wear their stripes."

June 19

Night stallion

"Mommy!" cries Christa in the middle of the night. "I had a horrible dream." "Never mind," soothes her mother. "You had a nightmare."
"A nightmare?" Christa thinks that's a funny name. "A mare is a mommy horse, isn't it?"
"Yes." Her mother nods.
Christa is quiet for a moment. She is thinking.
"A really bad nightmare must surely be a nightstallion!"
How funny. Christa and her mommy both laugh. All the horror is forgotten.

June 20

Horse talk

A horse, as we all well know,
Does not speak as humans do.
By one means or the other,
This clever animal converses.
It whinnies when it wants to call
And laughs to denote pleasure.
Words are quite superfluous –
Which means that they're not needed.
Snorting and blowing can convey:
"I like to be patted, but don't like working."

June 21

Never go to bed

Peter has been given a book about horses. He reads the whole book right away.
When he does not understand, he asks his mother and father. The book says that
horses do not sleep much. They take a nap now and then, and do not usually lie
down. "I wish I was a horse," sighs Peter, "And that Mommy was a horse."
"Why, sweetie?" asks his curious mother.
"Then I would never have to go to bed," Peter answers.

June 22

Schooling

It is not just human children who must go to school. Young horses also must be schooled and sometimes that can be an unhappy affair. Today, Darter is going to have a saddle on his back for the first time. "Bah! Ouch!" complains Darter. He bucks and rears. Let's get rid of that nasty thing! "Gently, Darter! Calm now, boy," soothes his owner. "The saddle is firmly fixed. You can't shake it off." After a quarter of an hour, the saddle is taken off. Upset, Darter returns to his mother. He tells her indignantly about what has happened. "You'll get used to it," promises his mother. "You'll soon not think anything of it."

June 23

Outlaw's horse

Trigger is a real outlaw's horse. His master is an outlaw. He robs banks and makes his getaway on Trigger. Clippity clop! They disappear before anyone notices.
The sheriff is puzzled.
No matter how quickly they chase the outlaw, they can never catch him. Even though the sheriff is a first-class tracker.
"He-ee-ee!" laughs Trigger. "My master is much cleverer than that sheriff. Do you know what he did? He had my horseshoes put on the wrong way around.
Back to front, do you get it?" Trigger thinks it's a huge joke. "The sheriff always searches in the wrong direction!"

June 24

Boasting

Richard turns up at school on his brand-new bike. He is very proud of it. He has been given it by a rich uncle – and it's not even his birthday!

"Look," Richard says. "This bike has twelve gears. It's the best bike in the whole world!"

Dan thinks Richard is always boasting. Of course, the bike is a good one, but he would rather have his pony.

"My pony can gallop very fast," he answers back.

"Oh, that old thing." Richard sneers. "I can go much faster on this bike."

Dan stops to think. He knows his pony is no longer so young. Then he begins to smile.

"At least my pony can never get a flat tire!" Richard has no answer for that.

Circus

"Come to the big top!" The circus is in town. There are posters everywhere.
"Greatest show on earth!" they proclaim. "Wild lions, giant elephants – come and see!"
Janet is going to the circus tonight with her mother and Dad. She is very excited.
"Will there be horses?" she keeps asking. Janet is crazy about horses.
"Wait and see," mutters her father. Janet drives him nuts about horses. But Janet cannot wait. She has to know whether there is an act with horses. She dreams of ten magnificent black stallions that perform the most amazing tricks.
"Oh, what a wonderful dream that was," she sighs.

June 26

Who dares?

Janet is at the circus with her parents. They have excellent seats right at the front. Janet is enjoying it. There have already been two horse acts and after the lions, there will be another turn with horses.

It is already starting. Men and women make fantastic vaults on the horses' backs as they canter around. And there are no saddles! Wait a moment, the music is stopping. One of the women takes a microphone.

"Is there anyone in the audience who dares to try riding one of these horses? Who dares?"

Janet jumps instantly to her feet. "Me! Me!"

Soon she is seated on a horse. First it walks around slowly, but then things speed up.

"Whee!" shouts Janet. "I want to work in the circus. This is fun!"

June 27

Slovenly

Jacqueline is very slovenly. If there is one thing she detests, it is being told to clean her room. That is when she loses everything. Yet she can be very tidy. Look at her pony's stable. Everything is kept orderly and clean. The grooming brushes are neatly put away. All the tackle is cleaned and polished.

But Jacqueline's pony is the dearest thing in the world to her. Jacqueline's mother often sighs when she looks in her daughter's room.

"I think I'd better put your bed in a stable. Perhaps you'd keep it tidy then."

"Hey, great!" shouts Jacqueline in glee. She pulls the mattress off her bed.

"Hold on, young lady!" her mother commands. "You surely don't think your pony wants to live with such a slovenly person as you!"

Lost

Katy has been grooming her pony for an hour. Once the pony is completely clean, she puts the saddle on her and then the bridle.

Samantha, her pony, begins to paw the ground in expectation. She knows that Katy is going to take her for a ride. She looks forward to trotting along the road. But where has Katy gone? Katy complains, Katy searches. Katy cannot find something.

"Where have I put my riding hat?" she asks. "Mommy says I'm not to ride without it. That is too dangerous. If you fall off without protection for your head, you can be badly injured." She continues to hunt for her hat. Samantha looks at her mistress. "Hee-ee-ee!" she whinnies. "Look in the mirror, Katy. What's that on your head?" Silly Katy is already wearing her hat. She'll never find it.

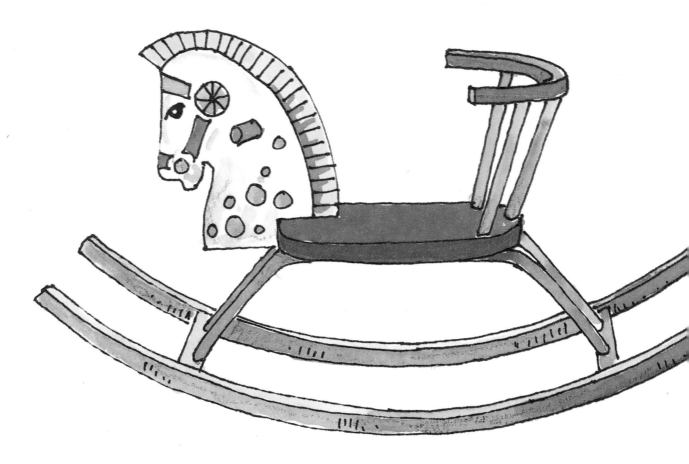

June 29

On the balcony

Stephen has a birthday. He is four years old. Hip hip hooray! Today he is finally going to get his birthday present. He has been talking about it for weeks. To everyone who asked him what he wanted, he gave the same answer: a horse. Stephen lives in a block of apartments on the twelfth floor. "Happy birthday to you…" sing his father and mother. "Here, Stephen, our present."

With curiosity, Stephen unpacks the present, already disappointed. It is a wooden rocking horse. With a glum look, Stephen says: "But I wanted a real horse!"

"But that's not possible, Stephen. You cannot keep a horse in an apartment."

"Of course I can!" argues Stephen. "He could live in my room and when he wants to go out, there's the balcony…."

124

Horse dealer

Off to the annual market
To buy yourself a horse.
You need to take great care
Not to buy some old nag, of course.
Is it young, or really old?
Should such a horse even be sold?
Is it kind and gentle natured
Or full of all the vices?
Check the horses carefully
And weigh all their prices.
A horse dealer is a businessman
And profit is his motive.
So good advice is, if you can,
Take someone with you who
knows horses. They'll be better
able to spot the wrong one
than someone like you, eager to
act on a whim. They might barter
so successfully that
all your savings might just buy the feed
for that horse you're after.

July 1

The Seaside

It is a marvelous summer's day. The sun shines in a clear, blue sky.
"Isn't it great, Mom!" whinnies Minnie the foal. Her mother nuzzles her behind the ears.
"Yes, it's nice in the summer," replies her mother.
"That's not what I meant," snorts Minnie. "I am happy that we live by the seaside and not somewhere inland. Now I can frolic in the sea when it is hot."
"At least we know she is not afraid of water." Her mother smiles.

July 2

Pony camp

The McFee twins go for a week to Pony Camp during vacation. They can ride every day they are there: Monday, Tuesday, Wednesday, Thursday…Then it is Friday.
"What a shame," says Jamie.
"Tomorrow's Saturday. We must pack up to go home." Fortunately, they still have the whole day. The leader has a wonderful surprise for them.
"Today we are going to take the ponies to the beach. You wait, you'll see how they love the sea."
"Yippee!" shout Lucy and her twin brother in unison.

July 3

Grays

Somewhere in France, far away, a herd of wild horses roams. They are beautiful horses. The stallions look like Arabs with long flowing manes and the same haughty proud looks. In the center of the herd is a small foal.
He is completely brown.
"How can that be, Mommy?" the foal wants to know. "You are white and Daddy is white," he says to his mother.
"Just wait," the mother assures the young foal. "We were all brown once. When you get bigger, you will change color. Then you will change from an ugly duckling into a beautiful white swan."
"I don't want to be a swan," grumbles the foal. "I want to be a stallion."

July 4

Your turn

Jewel is very fond of her master, Mark. Mark is very sweet. He is very patient and takes good car of Jewel. Every day Jewel is thoroughly groomed from head to hoof. Jewel likes this very much. Jewel would like to find some way to thank Mark for his care of her. But Mark does not understand horse language.
"Wait a moment," she whinnies, "You have groomed me so nicely, Mark. Now I will groom you."
With her lips, she plucks and sucks at Mark's hair. It leaves him soaking wet.
"Hey, stop that, Jewel!" shouts Mark. "You mean well but we use shampoo to wash our hair."

July 5

Smell

Before Irma's pony, Jamie, came to her, he was with a really bad master who beat and kicked the poor animal. That is why Jamie is still scared of people. However hard Irma tries, Jamie always shies away when he smells humans.
"What can I do to make Jamie trust me?" sighs Irma.
Her grandfather knows a great deal about horses. He has a plan. He explains it to Irma.
"Jamie is frightened when he smells humans. Put your riding clothes next to him in his stable. Then they will smell of Jamie. He's not going to be frightened by his own smell."

July 6

Scents

A horse is quite superior
In its ability to sniff,
But what a horse finds heavenly,
You might hate even a mere whiff.
Soap and perfume, it finds nasty
Perhaps to him, it's like a sewer
Filled with dollops of horse manure.
Yet for him the scent is heavenly.

Raspberry ice cream

Gypsy has an easy life. She does not have much to do. The whole year is spent in the meadow, except for the summer. Then her master drags a small cart out of his shed and puts Gypsy between its shafts. Together they go to the beach.
"Dingaling, dingaling" sounds the bell that her master rings. All the children hear the bell and know they are there. Patiently Gypsy waits until all the children have had an ice cream and then they move to another part of the beach. At the end of the day, Gypsy herself gets an ice cream. Her favorite flavor is raspberry.

July 8

Wasps

"I like my work," thinks Gypsy, the ice cream seller's horse.
"I spend the whole day on the beach. Lots of children come to see me. Of course the children all want an ice cream. But it's not only the children who are attracted by sweet ice cream.
"Bzzz, bzzz." A large black-and-yellow wasp buzzes close to Gypsy's ear.
"Buzz off! Horrible thing," whinnies Gypsy. The pony whisks her tail to ward off the wasp. The wasp angrily flies off. Oh dear, it has gone straight to a wasp's nest where all its brothers and sisters live. Let's hope that is not bad news for Gypsy.

July 9

Attack

A swarm of angry wasps is not very nice at all.
"Help!" scream the children who want to buy an ice cream.
"Help!" shouts the ice cream vendor. Everybody runs away from the wasps.
"What's the matter?" wonders Gypsy. The pony has not seen what caused the problem. She stands calmly with the ice cream cart. Until she is stung on the hindquarters.
"Hihihihihi!" screams Gypsy, galloping off with the ice cream cart behind her.

July 10

Happy fish

Gypsy looks around in astonishment. She is in the sea. Seagulls her is the ice cream cart. Cornets bob up and down in the waves. The sea is chocolate brown, strawberry pink and vanilla yellow. "Oh dear!" sighs Gypsy. "What a disaster. I was so shocked by that wasp sting on my bottom that I completely forgot about the cart." Here comes Gypsy's master. Thank goodness he is not angry with his pony! He is annoyed with the wasps. When he sees how glum Gypsy is, he makes a fuss over her. "At least the fishes will have a good day," he laughs.

131

Goliath

Police horses are both strong and brave. That is important because they often must do difficult and dangerous work. Goliath is a police horse. During his life he has carried a lot of policemen. But the years have passed and Goliath is getting older. His master is concerned about him.

"Goliath is too young to retire. He still enjoys working, but some of the younger horses go too quickly for him."

Goliath realizes something is amiss.

He whinnies softly: "Master, is there a problem? Can I help?"

Street organ

Goliath, the old police horse, looks up in surprise. A stranger has come into his stable. He takes Goliath with him. The large horse quietly follows him. Goliath is full of curiosity. What is up? There is a street organ outside his stable. The man turns the handle and…ta-ra-ra-boom-di-ay, the organ begins to play. Goliath does not flinch from the sudden noise. He has often seen a street organ.

"So, what do you think, Goliath?" asks the man softly. "Would you like to help me? Will you pull the organ through the streets?"

July 13

Dancing

There is a mid-summer festival in the streets of the village every year. All sorts of activities are involved: games for the children, a football match, a party in a huge hall and a parade.
Raffles is taking part in the parade this year. He must pull a cart full of children.
Raffles likes children. But Raffles likes parades even more. Do you know why?
"Don't those girls look lovely!" says Raffles. "Their costumes are very attractive and they do such clever things with their batons. And they dance so well."
Raffles also tries to dance. He lifts his legs up in time with the music.
"Look!" shout the people.
"That pony is dancing. Look how well he dances."
Everyone starts applauding.
Raffles is very embarrassed.

July 14

Vacation

Richard could almost cry. He must go on vacation with his parents. They are going to Spain for two weeks.

"What's the matter, Richard? Aren't you looking forward to the vacation?" asks his mother. "We are going to fly in a plane."

Richard is not to be comforted. He must be separated from his pony for two weeks. Sally must go to boarding stable for two weeks. With tears in his eyes, he says his farewells to Sally.

"Bye, dear, dear Sally," he sobs. "I hope they take good care of you."

Sally whinnies softly, as if she wants to say: "Don't fret, Richard. I'm going on vacation too. I am looking forward to two weeks with other horses."

July 15

No interest

Two weeks on vacation,
By air to sunny Spain,
Wonderful for some
But for Richard just a pain.
He cannot take his pony
With him to the sand.
It's not the kind of vacation
Richard would have planned.

July 16

New friends

At first, Sally missed her master a little. But after a few days at the boarding stable, she began to feel at home. She was well cared for and fed delicious pony treats. Because Sally is now calmer, today she may go in the field with the other horses.

"He-ee-ee, who are you?" she hears as soon as her hooves touch the grass. She is surrounded by horses. They have come to take a look at the newcomer.

"I am Sally and I am staying at the stable for two weeks," she tells the other horses. They understand her. The other horses like Sally. She is calm and does not want to be in charge.

"Let's be friends," suggest the horses. Sally nods in agreement. New friends, that's nice.

In her happiness, she forgets that she is supposed to miss her master.

135

July 17

Naughty rider

"Giddyup! Come on!" shouts Tom. Tom can ride quite well, but he is not very nice. If a horse does not go fast enough, he uses the whip. Sometimes he also kicks hard. Honeybee is no longer prepared to put up with it. The big mare bucks, rears and throws Tom off. "Good riddance," she whinnies in satisfaction. "If he doesn't behave, the only horse he's going to ride is a rocking horse."

July 18

Socks and shoes

"Clip, clop, clip…" Tiffany has thrown a shoe. When she walks along the street, you hear three hard sounds and one soft one. The blacksmith has been called out but until he can come, Tiffany's owner has removed another shoe.
Do you know why? It is because otherwise she would walk and stand unevenly.
Imagine if you had to walk in one shoe and one sock.
Now at least she can stand evenly on her hind legs.

136

July 19

Fancy dress party

Tonight there is a party at the riding
school. Because it is the summer
vacation, the people from the school
have thought up something nice.
Everyone can take part in a gymkhana.
But to take part you must come in fancy
dress.
Raymond rides his pony dressed like a
real cowboy. He has turned his riding hat
into a cowboy hat and he has tied a red
scarf around his neck. There is a lasso
on his saddle. Even his pony has been
dressed to look like a cow pony.
Raymond has dyed the white mane with
hair dye. Together they look quite
wonderful. Who knows, perhaps they
will win the competition.

July 20

Strawberries

It has been a very good year for strawberries. There are so many fruits on her
plants that Aunt Nell cannot eat them all. She plans to make jam with them.
The whole morning she has been busy picking strawberries. She has a bucket full.
"There!" she says, satisfied. "Just wash my hands and then these strawberries can
go into the preserving jars." But Aunt Nell has left the bucket foolishly close to the
fence. On the other side of that fence is Oliver the pony.
Sniff, sniff twitches Oliver's nose. "Mmm, that smells nice." When Aunt Nell
returns, the bucket is empty and Oliver's tummy is full. Fortunately, Aunt Nell
can see the funny side to it.
"It's my own fault," she laughs. "Besides, I much prefer plum jam."

July 21

Weather

Hail, wind and rain
Cause a horse little pain.
Backs against the wind they turn.
Foals too, quickly learn
To hide close to their mother
And horses shelter one another.

Raindrops no more pitter-patter,
And wind no more does chatter,
Whooshing through the trees.
There's light on the horizon.
Once more the sun comes here.

July 22

Thunderstorm

It is not always fine weather in the summer. Sometimes dark gray clouds appear in the sky. The horses in the field know that this means a thunderstorm. But when you are a tiny foal, you still must learn about thunderstorms.

"Hiiiiiiii!" whinnies Nirvana in terror at the first flash of lightning. The foal is very frightened. Then comes the thunder.

"Mamaaa!" he shrieks. He creeps as close to his mother as possible, shivering with fear. "Never mind," the mare soothes her foal. "The storm is a long way away. It makes a lot of noise, but there isn't any danger at the moment."

July 23

Greedy

Winny the pony is very clever, or at least she thinks she is. She has found a small meadow full of juicy, tender grass and she wants to keep it to herself. During the afternoon, when the other horses snooze, Winny slips away. She wants to keep that lovely, juicy grass to herself.
"Mmmm, this is definitely the tastiest grass I've ever eaten," says Winny as she digs in.
The sun in the sky looks down on Winny.
"What a greedy guts," the sun thinks. She makes him angry. And when the sun is angry, it becomes very hot. He aims his rays at Winny.
Oh dear, there's going to be trouble.

July 24

Sunburn

Winny spends the whole afternoon in her little meadow. In the full heat of the burning sun, she gluttonously feeds on the juicy grass. Horses can stand quite a bit of sun, but just like humans, they need to take care. Too much sun is also not good for horses. Too late, Winny thinks about the sun. Her whole muzzle is burnt.
"Ow! Ouch!" she whinnies. Quickly she trots to a brook. There she sticks her nose in the cool water. Her muzzle is so hot that the water sizzles.
Silly Winny – that's what comes of only thinking of your stomach!

July 25

Butterflies

Xaviera's field is filled with flowers.
There are red roses, white daisies, and
blue cornflowers. Xaviera loves flowers,
but not because they are pretty.
Xaviera gets her teeth into every flower
she sees.
"Hey, leave something for us!" says
a tiny voice. Surprised, Xaviera looks
around. Around her head flutter a pair
of butterflies.
"We must eat too!" cries one of the
butterflies. "We suck the nectar from
the flowers."
"I'm sorry, I didn't know that," says
Xaviera. "When you have sucked out
all the nectar, may I then eat the
flower?"

July 26

Two up

Sarah often stops to look at horses at the riding school. She finds the horses
wonderful, especially the piebald. One day Sarah says, "I would like to ride." The
very idea scares her. She wants to ride, but those horses are so big.
She is afraid. The man from the stable sees that she is frightened.
"I'll tell you what. I will climb up in the saddle and then you
can sit in front of me. Then nothing can happen."
Soon the two of them are riding around the ring.
At first slowly, and then at a trot. Sarah loves it!

Like on TV

Gerry has a plan. He wants to ride his horse to music, like he sees on the television. He takes the radio from his room to the field with him. It is fortunate that the radio is battery powered because there are no power outlets in the meadow. Soon Gerry is riding in circles. Everything goes well. His pony walks to the slow numbers. When there is a quicker number, his pony trots or canters. The music program is over far too soon. "We must do this again tomorrow," Gerry tells his pony, patting him on the neck.

Wild West

"Oh dear, oh dear," sighs Farmer Giles. "The fence is broken and my sheep have escaped." Charlie, the neighbor's son, is standing beside him. "I've got an idea," he says. "I'll fetch my pony. We can drive the sheep back into their own field." Immediately he sets to work. "Hi hi!" Charlie trots behind the sheep on his pony. "Hi hi!" He drives the sheep away from him. "Ba-aa," bleat the sheep as they run away from him. Farmer Giles watches in amazement, scratching his head under his cap. "Just like in the Wild West," he suggests.

July 29

Downpour

It has been dry and hot for several weeks. The leaves on the trees are hanging limply and the grass is arid and yellow. Tara the pony scratches at it. "It looks more like straw."

Her friend Sammy nods in agreement. "It's high time we had a good rain shower. That would be good for the grass and for us." Sammy glances at the sky. "Hey, look, Nature has heard us," he says, indicating the approaching clouds. Less than ten minutes later, it begins to rain. At first, there are gentle raindrops. But soon it is bucketing down. Tara and Sammy escape to shelter under the roof of the small building put there for just such a purpose.

"Mother Nature likes playing tricks. One moment it's as dry as a bone, the next soaking wet," complains Tara. Sammy shakes the water from his mane. "Gosh, what a downpour."

July 30

Not much room

At the far end of the field is a small stable of sorts. It has no windows or doors. It is more of a shelter. When it rains hard, the horses take cover in it. Not just the horses, though – also the sheep and the goat. But the shelter is too small for all these animals.

"Out of the way!" whinnies Fred as it starts to rain again.

"Baa-aa. We're allowed in here too," says the ewe.

"Baa-aa," wails the little lamb, as Fiona the pony accidentally shoves her.

"Sorry," sighs the pony as she helps the lamb to its feet. It is so busy in the shelter. Only Colin the goat is outside in the rain.

"The summer rain is good for the hair of my beard," he bleats. "It makes it grow."

July 31

It's raining

It's raining, it's pouring,
The horses are soaking wet.
Now they are sheltering,
Until the rain lets up.

August 1

Vacation

It is a glorious summer vacation for Rachel and Rebecca. Every day of the vacation finds the pair of them at the riding school, where they help look after the horses and have a ride.

"There's not even time to wash your jodhpurs!" complains Mom.

"See you this evening," shouts Rebecca. "Bye, Mom," calls Rachel. Once more they are off. Rachel and Rebecca are hardly ever home. Mom decides to talk to Dad about it. Yesterday she happened to see a nice pony for sale and she has an idea.

August 2

At last

"Girls," Dad begins that evening. They have just eaten. "Both of you know that Mommy and I would like to see you at home a bit more often."

"Yes, but..." Rachel interrupts.

"Just listen," interjects Mom. "We haven't finished. We know that you want so much to ride. And that you take good care of the horses at the stable. That's why your father and I have decided you can do so at home in the future."

"With your own pony!" adds Dad.

The children cannot believe their ears.

"A pony of our own? Really?" asks Rachel.

"All to ourselves?" asks Rebecca.

Mom and Dad nod yes.

"At last! Yippee!" both the girls scream. They do not know who to thank first, Mom or Dad.

My own pony

A pony of my own
Is what I dream of night and day,
A pony of my own,
For this I always pray.

A pony of my own
I would really care for,
I'd stroke it and I'd groom it,
And be very good to it.

August 4

Runny nose

Tommy is Miranda's pony. Miranda takes very good care of Tommy. Each evening, she brings him in from the field to the stable. Tommy has a fine stall next to two big horses. All in all, Tommy has nothing to complain about – and yet not everything is well with him. He always seems to have a runny nose.

"What's causing it?" Miranda asks the vet.

"It's not anything to worry about," replies the vet. "Tommy is allergic to being indoors. There is too much dust in these stalls. That's what has given him his runny nose. I suggest you open the outside vent in his stall every night so that he gets plenty of fresh air. You'll soon find his nose gets better."

August 5

Ergot

Two older girls are standing by the fence of the schooling ring. A lesson is under way. Young Peter also comes to look. The horses are huge. He can hardly believe his eyes. Then one of the girls points and remarks:
"Hey, look at the size of the ergots!" She points at the legs of one of the large horses performing an exercise. Young Peter looks puzzled, scratches his head and asks:
"What is big on that horse?"
"The ergots."
"But it is not a her, that's a him." The two girls laugh.
"No, no, Peter, I didn't say *her* had got anything. The knob at the bottom of the fetlock is called an ergot. I know that horse is a gelding, a boy horse."

August 6

A swimming pool full of potatoes

Bob takes Daffodil to a new field with his mother's help.
"The grass is really lush," his mother says.
"Daffodil will like that." Bob nods.
"We will must keep an eye on Daffodil or she'll eat too much. Given half a chance, she would eat so much that she would look like a large, round barrel.
It will be just like sitting in the middle of a big box of chocolates for her."
Mom is rather fond of chocolates. Bob thinks of his favorite food.
"It would be like swimming in a pool full of potatoes!"

August 7

A stable

Rachel and Rebecca have been given a really lovely pony by Mommy and Daddy. They are so happy. The pony is still with its previous owner because it has no stable yet. The pony can only come to live with them when they have a stable. Dad telephones the man who will build the stable.
"Can you put it up this week?" asks Dad. The man agrees.
First he makes the walls, the stable doors, windows and roof at his workshop. These are loaded on a truck. At Rachel and Rebecca's home, he quickly erects the stable in less than an hour. Now the pony can finally come to live with them!

August 8

Cleaning hooves

Karina knows how important it is to clean out her pony's hooves regularly.
That's why she tries hard to do the job thoroughly every day. Foxy, her pony,
does not like having his hooves scraped and when Karina attempts to, he keeps
his full weight on his hooves so that she cannot lift his leg.
"Foxy!" she says angrily to him. She pushes and shoves, but he will have none
of it.
Then Karina has a good idea. She must distract him. She immediately grabs
some hay and Foxy at once begins to munch it. Does it work? Foxy lets her lift
his hooves one at a time to clean them out.

August 9

Goat for company

Fanny is the dearest, sweetest horse in
the whole world, thinks her owner,
Tim. Tim is very, very fond of Fanny
and he goes to see her at least six times
a day. Fanny likes this, of course, but
when Tim is not with her, she is
lonely in her field. Fortunately, Tim
realizes this and has bought a little
friend for her from a farmer. It is
a goat kid.
"There you are, Fanny," Tim says.
"Now you don't have to be alone –
you've got your own goat for
company."

Mean horse

Bella, Björn and Buster are three Icelandic ponies. They live together in one of Farmer Bickerstaff's fields. They have a peaceful life. They graze a little, they trot a little and once a week, they take turns pulling Farmer Bickerstaff's trap. But today the farmer has brought a fine-looking black horse with him. "This is Zorro," he tells the other three horses. "He is coming to stay with you for several weeks. Be nice to him." Of course Bella, Björn and Buster will be nice to the new arrival. But, oh dear! He tries to bite them. Zorro wants to be the leader of the pack and to keep the best spot in the field for himself. So how can you be nice to such a mean horse? the other horses ask each other.

August 11

Invisible

Bella, Björn and Buster do not like Zorro. He tries to play the leader of the pack with them all the time.
"We must do something about it," sighs Bella to her friends.
"This cannot go on," agrees Björn.
"We were the first," grumbles Buster.
"Tell you what: I've got an idea," Bella explains. "Let's treat him as if he doesn't exist. For us, Zorro is invisible."
"This is a good idea. Soon the three Icelandic ponies stand with their backs to Zorro. If Zorro will not behave, he cannot be one of them.
It is his own fault.

150

August 12

Jumping

"Would you like to jump?" Wendy asks Mary.
They are outside in the school ring with Sooty the pony. Mary is too scared. She has never jumped.
"Sooty jumps really well," Wendy says proudly. "You'll see how easy it is."
"Okay," agrees Mary. "But only very low fences."
Wendy sets the rails to the lowest position.
"Just before you jump, you must stand up in the stirrups," she explains. Mary looks carefully. It certainly is a very low fence. First she puts the pony into a gentle canter. Sooty snorts. She knows what is coming – she is going to jump a fence. She runs at the fence, and then takes a huge leap over the obstacle. Mary is shocked and almost falls off.
"I told you so," laughs Wendy. "Sooty jumps really well. It's just that she likes much higher fences."

August 13

Soaring

My pony loves jumping high –
She truly comes to life.
High into the air she can fly,
Soaring like a lark that sings.
She cannot stay up in the air,
But would if she had wings.

Dawdling

Dobbin, the pig swill man's horse, spends whole days dawdling. His master too seems to have no desire to hurry. Dobbin jogs as slowly as possible from one house to another and people bring their vegetable peelings and other food remains to his cart.
When the sun starts to go down and they must go home, his master starts to think of his evening meal and Dobbin of his warm stable and fresh hay.
Then Dobbin lifts his head and begins to trot briskly.
Every evening, Dobbin is suddenly in a hurry.

August 15

To the woods

Rebecca and Rachel have had their own pony for a week now. She is called Fatima, which is an Arabic name, because Fatima is a full-blooded Arab. She is pleasant natured and very pretty and she loves to gallop.
For a week, the two girls have ridden their pony in the field, but they take her to the woods for the first time today. Fatima stamps impatiently.
Her nose has caught all the new smells in the woods.
Rachel only has to give her a nudge and she trots off eagerly.
"This is great!" she shouts to her sister. But Rebecca finds it rather creepy in the woods.
"I think in the future I'll stick to the fields," she says anxiously.

August 16

Bursting with energy

On Wednesday, Dick had no time to go riding because his friend had a party. On Thursday, Dick was a bit sick and on Friday, it rained. Finally on Saturday, Dick was able to take Whisper for a ride. In the meantime, Whisper has remained in the field, grazing grass or in her stable at night, where the box was full of feed.

In this respect, Whisper has not been neglected. Today, however, she is really eager for exercise. She can barely stand still and is raring to go. Soon Whisper is galloping pell-mell across the field.

"Whoa, girl! Steady!" Dick shouts, but it is quite useless.

Because Whisper is bursting with energy after so much grazing and oats.

An unusual present

Marcia is eleven today. That is quite grown up. Grown up enough, thinks her Grandma, for a very special present.

"Here you are, dear," says Gran, handing Marcia an envelope.

"Oh thanks, Gran," Marcia says without excitement. It will be some money or a book token.

"Open the envelope, Marcia." Grandma smiles. Something in the way Grandma says it makes Marcia curious. What could be so unusual in an envelope? There is a card inside with a pony on it.

"Best wishes," says the pony. Marcia then reads the rest of the card. "Dear Marcia, you are given a week at pony camp for your eleventh birthday present. Have lots of fun, Grandma." What a lovely surprise! Marcia is so excited that she is at a loss for words.

August 18

Pony camp

Pony camp has come at last!
Please, please let it be fun.
And make my pony very fast,
But also gentle natured.
Let's hope my fellow campers
Will turn out to be friends,
Sharing jam-filled doughnuts
Around a glowing fire.
Will pony camp turn out right?
Riding all day, and making lots of
friends each night?

August 19

Twelve Fjord ponies

Marcia had not slept for excitement. The day of the pony camp has arrived. There are twelve Fjord ponies, one for each of the twelve children at pony camp. Some of the other children have already arrived.
"Hi!" a boy calls to her. "I'm Charlie. It's great here, isn't it? Let's look around. What's your name?"
Marcia knows immediately that she is going to enjoy the week at pony camp. Together she and Charlie explore.
"This is Birgit. She'll be your pony," Charlie informs her when they reach the ponies. Birgit sticks her head out of her stall and begins to tug at Marcia's jacket with her lips.
"I think Birgit likes me already," Marcia laughs.

August 20

A card for Grandma

Marcia has had a wonderful time at pony camp. She decides she must send a card to Grandma to tell her all about it. The week's vacation was a present from Grandma. Marcia looks for a card with pictures of Fjord ponies on it. She chews the top of her pen and thinks about where to start. Should she describe the pony trek they made each day away from the camp or describe Birgit, her pony? What about all the mucking out! Would Grandma be interested in the disco? The card is far too small too write everything. So she writes: "Dear Grandma, it is fantastic here. I have a lovely pony called Birgit and we are going on lovely rides together. When I get home, I will tell you all about it, love and kisses, Marcia."

Stupid dog!

Matthew has both a pony and a dog. How lucky he is, you may think. But there is a problem. Patch the dog cannot get used to Pixie the pony. Every time Patch sees Pixie, he thinks she is a strange dog. She is very big, but she does not bark. She has a strange brush of a tail.
"Woof, woof!" He barks himself hoarse. But Pixie does not bark back. Patch decides to pull Pixie's tail to see if that will make her bark. Pixie does not like that at all. She has had enough. She lashes out with her hind legs and kicks Patch. Stupid dog!

August 22

Amanda has a birthday

Amanda has her birthday today and there is to be a birthday party. Not just any party, but a pony party. All her friends will go with her to the stable where she rides. Three ponies are ready for them to play great games with. There is a relay race, an egg-in-a-spoon balancing contest and a changing-clothes-while-riding contest.
What fun they all have! And what's more, the ponies enjoyed themselves too.
At the end of the afternoon, everyone is tired – children and ponies.
They will sleep well tonight – in their beds and stable.

Scooby doesn't want to!

It is evening. The red ball of the sun is slowly sinking behind the trees. Fran goes to collect Scooby, her pony, from his field. Scooby has had a wonderful day in the meadow. He has filled his tummy with fresh grass and tender buttercups. Scooby is still chewing when Fran comes with the halter to take him home. Scooby pretends not to hear her.

"Scooby! Come on, boy!" she calls. Scooby turns his large hindquarters toward her. He fakes deafness. But then he hears something rattling. What is that? Suddenly Scooby is no longer deaf. He can hear treats. He trots to Fran. After all, something sweet would make a nice change from all that grass!

August 24

Pony's birthday

Martina's pony, Jinty, has her birthday next week. Martina frets about what she can give her for a present. If it was for herself, she'd want a new Barbie doll, white riding breeches and riding gloves. But what can she give her pony? Fortunately, Mommy has an idea.
"Let's bake some pony biscuits with oatmeal. We'll add a little water and make a stiff dough. We then bake lots of little biscuits in the oven. Do you think Jinty will like her present?"

August 25

Playing in the hay

Freddie is a large, black Friesian. He is so enormous that he can be a bit scary. But Jake is not frightened of anything and anyway, Freddie is simply the nicest horse in the whole world as far as he is concerned. If Jake disappears, everyone knows where to find him – in Freddie's stall. Next to Freddie's stall there is a large pile of hay and Jake can find nowhere better to play. He makes a castle out of the bales and climbs up to the bars of Freddie's stall. Freddie watches the young boy the whole time and when Jake is close enough, he gives him a kiss.

August 26

Dazzler

Trudy, Troll and Tula, the three Fjord ponies, prick their ears when they hear Farmer Hagley's trailer pull up.

"Here you are, young ones. I've got company for you," Farmer Hagley calls to the three plain dun ponies as he lowers the ramp of the horse trailer. He leads a slim horse carefully down the ramp.

They look at it in surprise. Is that really a horse? A horse with black and white patches? The newcomer shakes his head wildly and sticks his nose in the air.

"What are you fatties gawking at?" he demands. "Have you never seen a cowboy horse before? My name is Dazzler and I am a Pinto. Our breed is all the rage."

What airs and graces! think the three quiet horses of Norwegian origin. They whinny: "How do they tell you apart from the cows?"

159

Horse show

There is going to be a horse show at the riding school, complete with a dressage trial. It will be next Saturday. Dick and Millie are practicing their routines and exercises every day. It is fortunate that they have their own pony. Dick runs through the routine with Millie before they start. Millie does exactly as Dick says – pirouette at *E*, change legs at *K*. Millie and Marmalade put every effort into doing well. Then it is Dick's turn. Marmalade gets double the practice. She can virtually do the exercise in her sleep. Soon Dick and Millie will not need to do anything; Marmalade will do it all for them.

Dreaming

I can do my dressage figures
With my eyes closed tight.
Each night in bed I ride the course
From *A* right through to *Z*.
Another fine pirouette,
Let's hope that when it matters,
I ride as well when I'm awake.

August 29

The great day

Finally the great day has arrived. Today is the horse show and the dressage trial. Dick and Millie were up early. Yet they have almost no time for breakfast because they must groom Marmalade. They brush her until she shines like a mirror. Then Millie plaits her mane into a hundred little plaits. When Dick and Millie appear in the dressage ring that afternoon, they steal the show. Not only are they superbly turned out, but they also ride extremely well. Marmalade is on her best behavior and she concentrates hard. Everybody applauds and they go home with a ribbon. They hang it on the door to Marmalade's stable. After all, it was she who really won the competition.

August 30

Not handsome, but sweet natured

There are all sorts of horses at the riding school stable: sweet-natured ones, mischievous ones and some that are downright badly behaved. Caesar, for example, throws everyone who rides him except the owner of the stables. The sweetest-natured horse in the stables is Rosinante. He looks nothing at all like the horse of anyone's dreams. He has crooked cow legs and a neck like a broom handle. His mane is like a bit of old string and his ears droop pathetically. In spite of this, Rosinante is the best horse in the stables. Even the most timid children are not afraid to ride him. "You are the sweetest-natured horse of them all," the woman who runs the school tells him each evening as she secretly gives him a sugar lump.

Rosinante

Long ago, in another country,
Lived errant knight Don Quixote.
Known for deeds of heroic gallantry.
Judging by his steed you'd think him crazy.
No braver man in all nobility,
Fought causes so forlorn and so lost.
The scraggly nag Rosinante's agility
And stout heart whatever the cost
Made him great in spite of his fragility.

September 1

Dreams

Luke dreams. He dreams the whole day. What is he dreaming of? He dreams that he is a famous rider. He wins all the big events on his horse. His trophy cabinet is crammed full of cups and ribbons. But Luke has not been going to riding lessons very long. Before he can become a champion he still has lots to learn. For the moment, he makes lots of mistakes.
"Luke, pay attention!" can be heard during his lessons. "Sit up straight! Heels down! Stop dreaming, Luke!"

September 2

Horse dreams

Do horses dream? If they do, do they dream of winning competitions and trophies? Jet the pony has quite different dreams. He dreams of a pretty mare. She is pure white with a long, black mane. Her eyes are jet black and they shine beneath long eyelashes.
"He-ee-ee," whinnies Jet in his sleep. In horse language that means: "I think you're lovely."
Perhaps Jet will really meet the mare of his dreams.

September 3

Apples

Buster grazes in an orchard full of sweet, tender grass. However, Buster prefers to pluck the apples off the trees. Soon the only apples left for the farmer to pick will be those that Buster cannot reach. But Farmer Hagley does not mind. The trees are old and even the cider factory no longer wants to buy their apples. If Buster did not eat them, they would fall to the ground and rot.

September 4

Snack bar

around and red
or sun bright yellow:
Trees are filled with apples
now that the days are
mellowing.
Pony looks, pony sees,
and scarcely believes
her eyes:
sweet snacks hanging ready.
This is pony paradise.

166

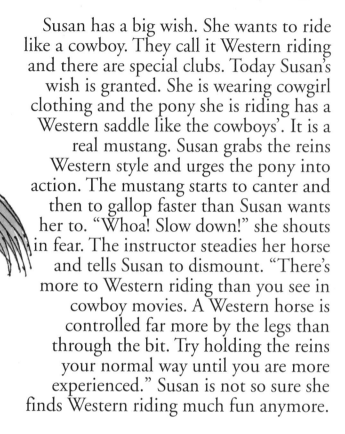

Cowgirl

Susan has a big wish. She wants to ride like a cowboy. They call it Western riding and there are special clubs. Today Susan's wish is granted. She is wearing cowgirl clothing and the pony she is riding has a Western saddle like the cowboys'. It is a real mustang. Susan grabs the reins Western style and urges the pony into action. The mustang starts to canter and then to gallop faster than Susan wants her to. "Whoa! Slow down!" she shouts in fear. The instructor steadies her horse and tells Susan to dismount. "There's more to Western riding than you see in cowboy movies. A Western horse is controlled far more by the legs than through the bit. Try holding the reins your normal way until you are more experienced." Susan is not so sure she finds Western riding much fun anymore.

September 6

Western riding

Susan now listens carefully to the instructor. She is learning the basics of Western-style riding. Riding Breeze alongside a fence, she learns to get the horse to move away from the obstacle with her legs. "Hey, it's like steering without using your hands!" "Glad you've got the message, Susan," says Darryl, who is instructing them. "A cowboy needs his hands for other things and a cow pony has to react quickly if it is to herd cattle. Now I'm going to show you how to put Breeze in reverse gear," he laughs. "But horses don't have gears!" "Actually we call it backing." Darryl draws the reins to him until his horse steps backward. At each step, he relaxes the reins and encourages his pony. When Susan tries, her pony does not seem to get the message. "Tap your leg against his shoulder on this side, Susan…" Her pony takes a backward step. "There, now you've found reverse gear."

Diesel

People often wonder why Diesel got his name. They guess it must be because he is a large, heavy horse who looks capable of pulling heavy loads. He has a strong body with enormous muscles in his stout legs. His hindquarters are almost the size of an elephant's. He is a very sweet-natured horse, but he does not know his own strength. When he gallops up to you it is wise to step aside. He careens around with flowing mane, causing a rumble in the ground. His large hooves dig up the ground and clods fly into the air. He is definitely a horse for heavy work. His owner calls him Diesel "because he's my spare tractor!"

September 8

Affectionate

Babs is crazy about her pony, Dancer. The spotty creature trots well and enjoys jumping, but Babs enjoys cuddling him most. She puts her arms around his neck and gently pets his mane.

"I could cuddle you all day," she whispers in his ear.

Dancer does not mind at all. He likes to make a fuss of Babs in return. He shoves his spotty muzzle against Babs and fumbles with her jacket with his lips. Sometimes he even bites it softly. But Babs knows Dancer is only being affectionate. Horses do that.

Prince

There is a new boy at the riding school. He is called Richard and has his own pony. It is a sweet fox red pony called Fawn. Richard is a nice boy with bright red hair and pleasant green eyes. What's more, he rides very well. When he is on Fawn, the two of them make a wonderful sight. All the girls think Richard is great. Brenda too. Indeed, Brenda is rather in love with him. She plays with her food at home and hears nothing of what is said to her. Brenda's parents know what's amiss.

"Let her be!" they say. "Brenda is dreaming of her handsome prince upon his horse."

Big girl

Antonia's foal is now four months old. She is old enough now to be separated from her mother.

"Come, Antoinette," says her owner, "we are going for a walk."

The foal whinnies softly. She wants to stay with her mother. Antoinette is difficult all the way to the new field, but she cannot resist. From now on, she must get by without her mother. Fortunately, there are other foals in the meadow. They are all the same age. They have each other for company.

Before he leaves her, the owner strokes her muzzle.

"Be brave," he tells her. "You're a big girl now."

September 11

Mama!

I want to go to Mama.
I am cold and I am tired.
With her I was protected.
She took good care of me.
She kept me safe from danger.
I am cold and I am tired.
I want to go to Mama!

September 12

Unicorn

There are many stories about horses.
Some are about very brave horses,
rescuers of humans. Some are about
sweet-natured or particularly
mischievous horses. There is also
a legend about a very special and
unusual horse: the unicorn.
The unicorn is sparkling white and has
a long, forward-pointing horn on his
head. His mane, tail and hooves are of
pure gold. The unicorn is a wild animal
that no one can tame. Do you believe
the unicorn really exists?

September 13

Washing line

It is a disorderly riding lesson. The children are chattering and giggling with each
other at the slightest provocation. Their riding instructor is rather impatient with
them. If the children will not listen, they cannot learn. But she does not want to
let herself become angry with them. Riding is something they do for pleasure. She
decides to try a joke on them instead. "Hey, kids!" she shouts. "Shall I fetch my
laundry basket and clothespins?" The children all look at her. They are
dumbfounded by her remark. "Yes," laughs the instructor. "Your reins are all as
slack as washing lines. I could hang my washing on them."

Best friend

"Caroline is my best friend," says Anna. "We enjoy the same things."
"Yes." Anna nods in agreement. "Except horses."
This is true. Anna is crazy about horses, but Caroline doesn't like them. "Horses smell, they rear, they buck and they bite," Caroline maintains. "What's so nice about that?"
Anna sighs. She is happy to explain but knows it will make no difference. "Never mind," she laughs. "You're still my best friend."

September 15

Giant

"Let me introduce myself," whinnies the very big horse. It is a very tall, strongly built, dappled gray. "Ee-aw, ee-aw," brays the donkey in the adjoining field.
"They call me François de Montparnasse. I am your new neighbor."
The donkey tries to repeat the name but fails. "What a mouthful. With a name like that, I suppose you must be somebody."
"I am a champion Percheron stallion. That's why I've got a French name. It is a bit much, I suppose."
The donkey laughs as he looks the long way up into the eyes of the gray horse.
"If you don't mind, I shall just call you Giant," he brays.

September 16

Golden coach

Willem is a Friesian heavy draft horse. He
lives in his native Holland. Willem is very
excited. Tomorrow he and five of his
cousins are going to pull the golden coach.
Willem knows they must be very careful.
It is not just that the golden coach is very
precious. Even more important is that the
Dutch queen will ride in the coach
tomorrow.
"I won't be able to sleep for nerves,"
he groans.
Silly, silly horse. If you don't sleep, you will
too tired to work. Then they will choose
another horse in your place.

September 17

Strange creature

"What's Jasper up to?" Edward asks his father in concern when they go to check
on his pony. Jasper is standing totally still in the center of the field. He sticks his
nose in the air and lifts his top lip. Then he gallops off and makes several circuits
of the field before repeating the same process.
Edward's father laughs.
"Jasper has discovered there is a new filly in the neighborhood. He can smell her
even at a distance. That's why he is behaving like that."
Edward shrugs.
"What a lot of fuss to make about a girl. What a strange creature."

September 18

Hiccups

Maritta is a Fjord pony.
She is usually calm as she walks slowly
along the road.
Almost nothing will upset her: cars,
motorcycles or even horns honking.
But one tractor upsets her terribly.
Then she bucks and rears and
misbehaves terribly.
There is no chance to get her to walk
properly back to the stables.
And she also gets hiccups that go on
for at least an hour.

September 19

Choke

Maritta is grazing quietly in the field. She looks for tender grass. Maritta knows what she likes and what she doesn't. But all the juiciest grass has been eaten. "Ah, there's a clump!" Her eyes fasten on a small remaining tuft. She walks toward it and sinks her huge teeth into it. Just as she is about to swallow, Farmer Hagley starts up the tractor.
"Hi-hi-hi!" she whinnies in terror with her mouth full. "Hic-hic-hiccup." Now she has swallowed the wrong way. She chokes. Until she clears the grass, she feels funny and clammy. Now she knows for certain – tractors are awful.

September 20

Fire

"Sniff, sniff," goes the nose of Helga the Haflinger. Haflingers are clever ponies from the Austrian Tyrol, who can quickly sense danger in the wild.
"Smoke!" smells Helga. "Fire!" she knows. "Danger!" she screams. "Let's get out of here," she shouts. But Helga is not out in the wild; she is in a stable. The stable door is shut. The cows and sheep that are also in the building with her are terrified.
"Don't panic, Helga," she tells herself. "You've got strong legs and hard shoes. You'll soon have that door open." Quickly she kicks the door open – not a moment too soon – for the flames are blazing all around.
Thanks to Helga, all the animals are able to escape.
"Thank you, Helga," moo the cows.
"Thank you, Helga," bleat the sheep.

September 21

Wind

It is autumn. The leaves on the trees are changing color. They are beautiful reds and yellows. Some have even started to fall. They provide fun for the autumn wind.

"Whoo-oooo," whistles the wind as it chases the leaves. Conker the stalwart stallion looks a bit uneasy. Every time he goes to take a munch of grass, the wind blows dead leaves in front of his nose.

"Bah!" complains Conker. "How's a horse to eat? Stop it, you naughty wind!"

But the wind does not stop. It finds the game such fun.

September 22

Autumn

Dead leaves and strong winds
Mark when autumn begins.
Soon there'll be no more grass,
Or sunny grazing days to pass
In the meadow along the way.
Now it will be a diet of hay,
And a stable for the winter.

September 23

Whiskers

Whiskers the cat has come to take a look
at the field. The horses are all standing
snoozing. Whiskers begins to groom her
whiskers, making sure they are straight
and clean. Tinkerbell the pony is curious
and comes to have a look.
"What beautiful whiskers you have," she
says to the cat.
"Yes," agrees the cat. "But they are useful
too. I can feel things with them."
"I've got hairs like that too," says
Tinkerbell, "especially under my chin."
Whiskers takes a good look. "Well,
I never! So you have. But in your case,
it's a full beard."

September 24

Green horse?

Stephen is in seventh heaven. He is to have a pony as a present from his parents.
Yippee! Stephen wants to go to look for a horse immediately. His parents take him
to the auction where horses are being sold. The horse dealer asks:
"What sort of horse are you looking for? A quiet animal that is well schooled?
Or perhaps you'd rather have a green horse?"
Stephen is taken aback. A green horse! Most definitely not!
"I want a lovely chestnut."
The dealer throws his head back and roars with laughter.
"A green horse is not green in color. It is an unschooled novice. But I think that
you'd be better with an experienced horse."

September 25

Maize

Rosie's field is surrounded by fields full of maize. The stalks are easily six feet high and they bend under the weight of the corn cobs.

"Bah!" says Rosie. "Maize to the left of me, maize to the right of me and maize front and back." She hates the lack of a view. She can no longer see who is coming along the road. In her anger, she starts to bite the corn.

"Mmm, that tastes good!" Rosie has bitten into the cob. It not only tastes delicious, it is also sweet.

"Ahem! I think that perhaps being surrounded by maize fields is not so bad," she says between bites as she smacks her lips.

September 26

Dirty devil

Karen knows that you must take good care of your pony. That's why she gave extra-special attention to grooming Piccolo today. His coat shines.

"There, Piccolo, you look lovely again," Karen says, standing back to admire him. "Now you can go out to graze." Piccolo is looking forward to that. He canters to the center of the field and finds a muddy patch of ground. Then he rolls over in the mud!

"Oh, Piccolo! How could you?" screams Karen. "Look at you, you are filthy! I only just got you clean. You dirty devil!"

September 27

Grumpy

The children at the riding school all seem to be grumpy today. The boys are grumpy with the girls and the girls are grumpy with the boys. It seems as though a storm is brewing. Charlie, the riding instructor, is fed up with them all.

He complains: " If you must grumble at each other, try to be a bit nicer. Don't call each other fools, but something like doughnuts."

It worked. A doughnut on a horse – how funny!

"Hey, bag of chips, get out of the way!" was soon heard. Or, "Bar of chocolate, move aside!"

Soon the children are no longer grumpy with each other. All the stupid names have made them all happy again.

Wild horses

Horses are very useful animals. You can ride them or they can pull a coach or cart or they can plow the land. But wild horses do not work. They live together in herds and look out for themselves. Khongor is a wild horse. His coat is light and tan colored and his mane sticks up like bristles. He uses his dark, shining eyes to keep an eye open for danger. Wild horses are very wary. They trust nothing and no one. Khongor trusts people least of all. People try to catch you. Then they put a sort of chair on your back and sit in it. It gives him the shivers to think about it.

"If they try that with me, I will throw them off immediately."

September 29

Name

Geraldine does not like her name. When people shorten it, it is no better, she thinks. She imagines she is stuck with her name. Fortunately, her pony has a lovely name: Bianca. That rolls off the tongue better than Geraldine. "Bi-an-kaaaa!" she calls her pony, letting the last syllable run on. She thinks of their names together. "Gerry and Bianca? Yuck! Bianca and Gerry? That's slightly better. But she likes the ending better of her pony's name. Then it comes to her. "I'll ask everybody to call me Dena." She pronounces it *dean-a*. "Dena and Bianca!"
She is so happy with her new name, she starts to sing it.

September 30

Tone

A horse is quite unconcerned
Whether you call him Beauty,
Danny Boy or Scooby Doo.
He's really not that snooty.
Pixie or Honeybee,
Lady, Buster or Pattacake.
They couldn't care a jot.
A name is just the sound you make
When you call him.
If you use a friendly tone,
He'll answer just the same.

October 1

Migrating birds

"Honk, honk, honk," sounds in the air above the meadow. Cloud, the slender horse, looks up. He sees a large flock of geese landing.
"Hey! What's that?" he snorts in surprise.
"They are coming to my field."
In no time at all, the field is full of geese. The birds eat the grass. That is not good! Cloud approaches them with determination.
"He-ee-ee," he whinnies. "Leave my grass alone." A large gander is not scared of Cloud. He spreads his wings and squawks back:
"We are not going yet. We must eat before we fly away somewhere warmer a long way away and we would not make it if we did not eat first. Do you mind if we have some of your grass?"
"Of course not," whinnies Cloud in reply. "Just keep everything tidy."

October 2

Flying horse

With a great sound of flapping wings, one after another, the geese depart. Soon they are flying in a large V formation over Cloud's field. The pony wonders at the sight.
"Mmmm," mumbles Cloud. "I wish I could fly too. There is enough room on my back for a few geese. It must be wonderful to fly through the air."
When Cloud snoozes a little later, he imagines himself flying high above the clouds with great flapping wings. Cloud the flying horse.
"If I could fly," he says to himself, "I could spot the best patch of grass."

Hundreds and thousands

There is a new pony in the field. He is white with chocolate markings all over his body. The other horses ask the new pony his name.

"Hundreds and thousands," the newcomer explains.

"That's a strange name. What's the meaning of it?" ask the other ponies.

"Hundreds and thousands are decorations that they put on children's puddings and cakes for parties. I'm called that because of all my chocolate spots."

October 4

Appaloosa

Martin's mother has taken him to see the new pony, Hundreds and Thousands, in the field near their home.

"He is an Appaloosa," says his mother.

"Why does it keep losing apples, Mommy?" Martin asks. He wonders whether he should give the pony the apple he has brought for it.

"Not apple loser, Martin – Appaloosa – it is an American breed. They were bred by the Indians." Martin offers the pony his apple. He takes the apple from his hand and it disappears immediately into the pony's mouth. In one crunch, the apple is gone. "It is an apple loser after all, Mommy. It lost that apple pretty quickly." Martin's mother laughs at her son's joke.

October 5

Acorns

Autumn
Is the time of year
When the acorns fall.
Plop, plop, they drop
Down to the ground
Or onto a pony sheltering
Beneath the huge oak tree.
An acorn might hurt a little
But it could, of course, be worse
For inside every acorn
There's a new oak in the making.

October 6

Clunk

Clunk, clunk, thud. Strange sounds are coming from underneath the oak tree.
Serena the pony has been hearing the sounds all day. She decides to take a look
to find out what is causing them. Clunk, she hears beside her, clunk, clunk she
hears behind her.
"Brrr," snorts Serena. "Is there a spook here that goes clunk?"
She searches among the grass, but all she finds are small brown things. Then
"clunk" really close.
"Ouch!" Serena jumps. An acorn has fallen on her head.
She takes off like a hare. She does not like these clunk spooks that fall on her
head.

October 7

Trio

The three Shetland ponies are inseparable. All three are equally small, brown and hairy.

Uncle Charles takes his nephew John with him to their field. "Come along to see the three brothers."

"What three brothers?" John asks. When he sees the Shetland ponies, he understands.

"Do you have any idea what to call them?" asks Uncle Charles.

John barely pauses to think.

"What about Mickey, Donald and Pluto?" Uncle Charles laughs.

"I should have guessed. It's all you think about since you've been to Disney World."

October 8

Hardy pony

Brr, it is very cold and wet. It has been raining and blowing a gale all day. Sally thinks it is time to bring her pony in from his field. She opens the stable door and calls him. "Viking, come on, Viking!"

Viking is well aware that he will must go into his stall. That is why he has remained at the far end of the field all day. He does not like being shut up in the stall. He finds it nicer out-of-doors. His thick winter coat protects him from the cold. He is a hardy pony.

"She can call as long as she likes – I'm not coming," Viking snorts.

After a quarter of an hour, Sally gives up. He will must decide for himself.

October 9

A horse with a jacket

Not all owners take the same care of their pony. Fred's owner leaves him out-of-doors no matter how heavily it rains. Fortunately, Fred can cope with living out-of-doors. Fred is also clever. When it starts to rain, he stands under the trees for shelter. But today, he notices that even under the trees he is getting wet. He gets a big surprise when he looks up. All the leaves have gone from the trees. The raindrops fall straight through the bare branches. Fred does not like it.
"Ahem! I shall speak to my owner about this," he grumbles. "If he does not do something about those leaves, I will take his jacket from him."

October 10

Rubber boots

Most horses do not mind a little water. In the summer, it is even welcome because it cools their legs. But Ryan has an absolute hatred of getting his feet wet. When his owner rides him, he skirts right around puddles. Sometimes, though, they are too big to avoid. Then he refuses to budge.
"Walk on, Ryan!" demands his rider. "Surely you aren't afraid of getting your feet wet?"
Ryan looks annoyed. It is all right for his rider to say that when he is wearing rubber riding boots that keep his feet dry.
"He-ee-ee!" protests Ryan.
"Buy me some rubber boots and you'll see how quickly I go through water."

Horse's eyes

If you ask Naomi why she likes horses
so much, she always says:
"Because of their eyes."
Naomi thinks horses have the most
beautiful eyes in the whole world. They
are very big and loving and they often
have very long lashes.
"Look at sheep's or goat's eyes," she
suggests. "They are nowhere near as
pretty. Our dog looks intelligent but he
does not have those long lashes."
Naomi strokes her horse's head.
"If I talk to Fanny, she looks as though
she understands everything I say."
Fanny listens to Naomi's voice and
gives her a wink.

October 12

Accident

That silly boy, Gary. He insists on riding bareback. He mounts his pony and
grabs it by the mane, shouting: "Giddyup!"
His pony is surprised and bucks. Gary is not prepared for this. He flies
through the air and lands on the ground with a loud thud.
"Ouch! Ow!" His shoulder hurts a great deal. He has to go to the hospital.
The doctor finds that he has broken his collarbone.
"You'll be in a sling for six weeks," the doctor explains.
"Six weeks like this! I won't be able to ride!" realizes Gary.
Poor Gary, he is being doubly punished: a painful shoulder and no riding for
six weeks.

October 13

Toadstools

They say that horse manure is very good for growing mushrooms and toadstools. If you take a look in Speedy's field, you may think that is true. There are small groups of toadstools everywhere among the grass. Speedy does not fancy eating either mushrooms or toadstools. He gives them a wide berth. But now and then he goes to stand close to them. Then he tilts an ear toward them and listens carefully. Speedy has heard that elves live in toadstools and Speedy wants to see an elf. He has no luck, though. Not a single elf ever comes out of any of the toadstools.

"Humpf," he snorts. "I don't think elves exist."

October 14

Storm

There's a storm blowing
Waves toss house high
The danger's ever growing
Though you don't hear the seaman cry.

A ship in peril looming
Helpless before the blast
tore away her rigging
And carried off the mast.

The shore's in view;
Strong horses toil and strain
To help the brave lifeboat crew
Launch the lifeboat from its train.

October 15

Maroon

There is great commotion on board the *Nelly III*. The skipper and his two
crewmen are pumping water out of the vessel. But it is not helping much.
The gale blows yet more water into the ship. Soon the *Nelly III* will sink. On shore
in the lighthouse, the keeper has seen the danger and he fires the signal flare. The
lifeboat must go to sea to save the three sailors. With the storm whistling across
the coast, horses must be taken from their warm stables. They must pull the
lifeboat to the sea. It is a difficult job and not every horse is suitable. The lifeboat
horses are strong and brave. They are also dependable.

190

October 16

Heroes

Matthew and Mark, Luke and John, Timothy and Simon, Peter and Paul. These are the names of the strong geldings of the lifeboat team. These horses often must go out when there is a storm outside and other horses are safe in a warm stable. Matthew and Mark are the leading pair. They are not afraid of high waves. Luke and John follow.

The salty water in their nostrils makes them snort. Timothy and Simon docilely follow Luke and John. They dig their large hooves into the sand. Peter and Paul bring up the rear. Behind the horses they drag the lifeboat over the sand on its frame. The eight horses defy the danger. The lifeboat is able to save people thanks to them.

Many mariners owe their lives to them.
The horses are true heroes.

Spider's web

Across the stable window
A spider's web is spun.
The pony is contented with
The new curtains she has won.

October 18

Fly catcher

There can even be flies and spiders in the autumn. Tamar the pony has had enough of them. The nasty creepy crawlies can go to the moon as far as she is concerned. Look, there is another creepy thing! Tamar snaps at a small spider.

"Hey, hey!" shouts the spider.

"I didn't do anything. Why do you do that?"

"You are a nasty creepy crawly," complains Tamar. "You are going to pester me just like all those horrid flies."

"No, I won't!" says the spider emphatically. "I catch flies in my web and then eat them all up."

"Oh! That's a different matter," says Tamar.

"If you will keep my stable free of flies, I will make sure your web is unharmed. Such a fly catcher will be very useful."

192

October 19

Expensive?

Ellen has bought a pony with her own pocket money. She does not intend to ride her pony. She is much too small for a big girl.
No, Ellen wants to look after the pony.
Fortunately, Ellen lives on a farm. Her father has more than enough grass in his meadows, so her pony has plenty to eat. In the winter, her pet can have some of the cow's hay.
Her school friends sometimes ask her: "Do you really have your own pony? Isn't that expensive?"
Ellen laughs at them. "Not if your father is a farmer!"

October 20

Feathers

Johnny's father is a horse dealer. Today, Johnny is going with his father to look at a horse. Before they go to the stable, the owner and his father talk about the horse they have come to see. "He has excellent conformation with abundant feather," says the man to his father. Johnny is astounded. He has grown up in a family that deals with horses and he has never, ever seen a horse with feathers on it. All the horses Johnny has seen have coats of hair. What kind of horse is this one? He joins his father in the stable, full of curiosity. But he can see no feathers on the horse. It is a huge, heavy horse. "But Dad, it hasn't got any feathers at all!" he says. The two men laugh.
"Not feathers, Johnny," says his father, pointing to the long hair at the bottom of the horse's legs. "Feather, or feathering – that's what they call this hair at the bottom of the legs."
Johnny goes bright red at his silly misunderstanding.

Hunting

The hunting season has started. The hunting horns trumpet their call. The dogs bark and are eager to get going. The horses snort and rake the ground with their hooves. Everyone watches for the signal. Bailey the hunter has his ears pricked. His rider is a very genteel woman. She is the Honorable Cecilia Ponsonby-Smythe. The Hon. Cecilia does not like hunting. She does not approve of blood sports and feels sorry for the fox. Fortunately, this is a drag hunt – a scented bag is chased instead of a fox. Bailey knows that his mistress does not enjoy hunting. She always dawdles and lags behind. Bailey thinks that is a shame. He wants to be up at the front. Once the master gives his signal, Bailey shoots forward.

"Oh dear!" cries the Hon. Cecilia. "I'd really rather ride at the rear."

October 22

Ditched

Ge-de-dunk, ge-de-dunk, ge-de-dunk thunder the hooves of Bailey the hunter. The poor Hon. Cecilia is shaken to the core as she clings on grimly. Ge-de-dunk, ge-de-dunk! The rhythm of the hooves speeds up as Bailey chases after the hounds. The Hon. Cecilia is so scared that she has closed her eyes. But you cannot see anything with your eyes closed. She cannot see the ditch in front of them. Bailey quickens his pace still more to a run and makes an enormous jump. He lands safely on the other side. But where is the Hon. Cecilia? She is no longer on his back.

October 23

Honorably damp

The Honorable Cecilia Ponsonby-Smythe has fallen off her horse during the hunt. Soaking wet, she sits in the ditch. Her hair is full of duckweed and there is a frog sitting on her head.
"Rivet," croaks the frog.
"Yuck!" screams the Hon. Cecilia.
"He-ee-ee," whinnies Bailey the hunter. "What's keeping you? The hunt is getting away."
The Hon. Cecilia has no more interest in hunting. She wants to get home as quickly as possible to change into dry clothes. She takes hold of Bailey's bridle and leads him back home. Disappointed, Bailey follows her. Now he won't be in the lead anymore.
"Better luck next year," she consoles him. "But at least we caught a frog."

Collection

Sarah lives in an apartment. She lives right on the top floor. From her room she can see the whole town, or at least she could if she looked out of the window. But Sarah prefers to look at the walls of her room. They are covered from floor to ceiling with posters of horses. Galloping horses, grazing horses, huge horses and foals. Sarah collects everything that has to do with horses. The only thing missing is a real horse.
"I couldn't have one in an apartment," she laughs. "But later, when I am grown up and have earned lots of money, I will buy my own horse. Then my collection will be complete."

October 25

Black and white

Nigel is a little boy who loves to wear black because he thinks it makes him look like Zorro from the old movies that his grandmother watches. So he wears black riding breeches, a black shirt, black boots, a black cowboy hat and a long black cape. The other children stare at him every day at riding school. But Nigel does not mind. His favorite horse is Snowy, the almost pure white gray. If he rides Snowy, her whiteness contrasts beautifully with his black riding clothes and he looks very dramatic. The other children say he looks like a chessboard.

October 26

Getting fit

There is soon to be an important trial for young riders. Marianne has entered herself. She intends to win. But to win, it is essential to practice. How can she practice every day when she does not have her own horse at home? But Marianne has an idea. There is a large area of grass in the park next to their house. She has written down on a scrap of paper what she must do for the trial.

"Now I'd do everything as though I was on a horse," she tells herself. She holds her hands in front of her as though she is holding the reins and she begins to pace. She runs as if she were trotting and to gallop, she tries to keep her legs in the correct position. She practices all afternoon like this until she has memorized everything.

"Well, Marianne," says her mother with a big smile, "whatever happens, you'll be pretty fit for the trial."

Playing

Poppy the pony is put in a stall every night. It is nice and warm in the stall and there is always ample hay. As soon as Poppy is in her stall, she begins to munch the hay. But after a while, her belly is full. "Ah," sighs Poppy. "The night has hardly begun and I don't need to sleep." She is rather bored. She looks around for something to do.
"Hey, what about that?" She stretches out her neck as far as she can reach and with her lips pulls one of the brushes out of the bin where they are kept. "Thud," the brush falls to the floor. What a fun game. She is happy for hours. When her owner comes to collect her in the morning, the grooming equipment is spread all over the floor.

October 28

Chewing

Twiglets is a good horse. She is very good with children, she likes to work and never bucks or rears. She only has one vice. She can't stop chewing. She chews all the wood in sight – the fence in her field, the stable door and also the window.
"You are more of a beaver than a horse!" complains Mr. Richards, her owner. He is constantly having to repair the fence and the stable door. Confused, Twiglets nudges his shoulder.
"Don't be angry, Master," she wants to say.
Fortunately, Mr. Richards is not really angry. But to be sure, he caps the stable door with metal.
"You won't manage to chew through that," he laughs.

October 29

Bunny and the hare

A pretty chestnut mare is in the field. It is quite early. Most people are still sleeping. The wild animals still dare to put in an appearance at this time of day. That includes the hare family.

"Good morning," says Dad Hare to the mare. "Lovely weather for the time of year." He hopes to have a conversation.

"What's your name?"

"Bunny," answers the mare.

"Bunny? Isn't that what people call rabbits? Are you a distant relative?"

The mare chews until her mouth is empty and looks at the hare, somewhat surprised. This lowly creature a distant relative?

"Oh no!" she whinnies. "It is a children's pet name for me. My full name is far too much of a mouthful."

October 30

Legless horse

Mist hangs over the field. Fifi the foal wakes up and blinks. She has never seen mist before.

"Mama, what is it?" she cries softly to her mother. Then she gets the shock of her life. Her mother is standing there, but without any legs. She seems to float on clouds of cotton wool.

"Mama! The wolf has eaten your legs during the night," Fifi screams. Somewhat surprised, her mother looks up.

"No, my little child. I've got all four legs. You just cannot see them because there is a sort of cloud hiding them. Come closer, you'll see everything is all right. Besides, there aren't any wolves around here, sweetheart."

October 31

Mist

In the mists of autumn,
When the weather's fine
Horses lose their legs
And float on fluffy clouds
Like huge white sheets
With horses' heads.
Then only the horses' backs
And tails can still be seen
Above the mist, like an illusion.
Headless horses' hindquarters
Are grazing in the meadow.

November 1

Cold

"Brrr!" Sadie is shivering on the playground. She hopes the bell will ring soon so that she can go indoors. It is no fun to be outside when it is so cold. Then she is shocked to remember that her pony Trixie is still outdoors. Surely Trixie will be shivering from the cold. Now Sadie is no longer interested in getting indoors to the warmth. She wants to go home to Trixie.
It seems ages before she can go home. She hopes her mother will come to pick her up soon. She can think of nothing else all morning than her poor Trixie outside in the cold.

November 2

Wrapped up

What can you do to beat the cold? Sadie remembers. You put on warm woolen clothing, wear a scarf and put a hat on your head. Can a pony also wear such things? Sadie has dug out some old clothes for her pony Trixie. She can protect her pony from the cold, she thinks. She quickly ties a scarf around Trixie's neck, but the hat is a problem. It keeps falling off. She has an idea and cuts out holes for Trixie's ears. Now the hat stays in place.
The long kneesocks are ideal for Trixie's legs. A little later, Sadie's mother comes to look. She dissolves in a fit of giggles.
What a strange sight – Trixie wearing a hat and socks!

Wooden Horse

Eric's mother is dumbfounded. Eric is visiting the neighbors yet again – and they do not even have any children! She wonders what he does there. She puts her coat on and goes around to the neighbors.
"Good afternoon," she says as the neighbor's wife answers the door. "Do you find it a nuisance if my son wants to play around here all the time?"
"Certainly not!" answers the neighbor.
"He is so sweet. Come and look." Eric's mother follows her through to the living room. Eric is on his knees. He is playing with a beautiful wooden horse. Now Eric's mother understands. "Eric is crazy about horses," she explains.
"And I am crazy about children," laughs the neighbor.

November 4

Fabiola

Fabiola the wooden horse
Has a silk mane and a silk tail.
Saucily she lifts a leg
As if she wants to gallop.

Fabiola looks like a treasure
With her gleaming coat of paint.
So marvelous that does it matter
That she's not a real living horse?

November 5

Inquisitive

The blacksmith is visiting. He is making new horseshoes for Parker
the pony. "So, horse," says the blacksmith as he taps her shoulder,
"you're gettin' new shoes today, girl." Parker is quite happy. The blacksmith
has a marvelous scent of horses and he has lots of interesting things with him.
Each time he picks up a different tool, she tries to get close to take a look. She
wants to sniff everything. The black smith finds it a nuisance. When the new
shoes are all finally in place, he takes a breath and tells Parker: "Now I know
where you got your name. You're a nosy little thing, ain't you?"

November 6

Licked

Tamara has gone with her father to
look at the horses. She has taken a bag
of stale bread and some bits of carrot
with her. As soon as she is by the fence,
the horses trot over to her.
Crunch, chew, slobber, slobber. The
horses like the tasty snack. The bag is
soon empty. Tamara then wants to
stroke one of the horses' noses.
"Help!" she cries out. "He wants to eat
my hand."
Daddy must laugh. "Horses don't eat
meat, darling. I think your hand still
smells of carrot. The pony just wants to
lick your hand. Hold your hand out
flat. Then he can't bite it."

Counting

Jimmy is crazy about counting. He counts everything he sees. Two sandwiches on his plate: one, two. Three birds on the washing line: one, two, three.
Now Jimmy wants to count the horses in the field. He begins: one, two, three…but then the horses move. Jimmy immediately loses count. Which horses has he counted already and which hasn't he?
Jimmy starts again: one, two, three, four…and now all the horses change around again. Will Jimmy ever manage to count them? His mother suggests something. She tells him: "Every horse looks different. Look, that one has a white nose and the others have white manes."
A little later, Jimmy knows that there are seven horses in the field: one, two, three, four, five, six, seven.

Strange horses

The baker in the village comes up with something new every week. Sometimes he sells acorn rolls. They really look like an acorn. Other times, he bakes sticky fishes – sticky buns in the shape of a fish. This week, he has come up with something special. He has made cookie horses. But that is not so easy. A horse is difficult to make. One time, the legs are crooked, the next, the heads more closely resemble pigs.
"Bah," sighs the baker. "Horses are far too difficult for me." But he has an idea. That afternoon, a board hangs in the bakery. On it is written: "Cookie monsters, thirty-five cents each."

November 9

Thief

Now that the evenings are getting darker, Tina can no longer take such good care of her pony. It is darker in the stable than outdoors. So her father has installed a lamp in the stable.

"Thanks, Dad," Tina tells her father that evening at supper. "At least I can now see what I am doing."

"But the lamp is still on, Tina," her father scolds her. Tina cannot understand. She knows for certain that she switched the lamp off. Could there be a thief in the stable? She goes to see with her father. Suddenly the lamps goes out… and then on again. Guess who is doing it. Tina's pony has found she can switch the light on and off with her lips. She thinks that is a grand game.

Now Tina's father is going to put in a light switch where the pony cannot reach it.

November 10

Pepper

Brian's horse is called Pepper. But Brian prefers to call him Peppie. Brian cannot stand pepper on his food. The horse was called Pepper when he came to Brian. It seemed best not to change the horse's name too much.

Pepper does not mind what Brian calls him so long as he continues to be nice to him and goes on taking good care of him.

He will answer to Brian's kind voice. He knows that when he comes to Brian there is never a nasty surprise.

Now that Brian is getting to know Peppie better, he thinks his horse's new name is ideally suited to him. He has so much pep, thinks Brian.

November 11

Running

Running, running
Galloping like the wind
Pepper thinks what great fun it is
Galloping to the end of his field
And back again.
This horse's legs
Run really fast
To and fro
And around the barn.
Pepper is enjoying
A quick, crazy moment.

November 12

Freezing rain

What a disappointment! Brian wants to ride his horse, Pepper, but the ground is
like a skating rink. It has been raining and the rain freezes when it hits the ground.
Pepper could slip and fall and break a leg. Fortunately, a truck spreading salt comes
along the road. Brian knows that the truck is spreading salt to melt the ice.
"Hey, that's an idea," Brian says. "I'll ask them if they can spare some salt. Then
I can spread it on the ground."
The men in the truck are in a good mood. They let Brian have a bucket of salt.
Soon Brian is busy spreading salt on the ground. He laughs as he does it at
a thought that has entered his mind. He beams at his own joke.
"When we ride after I have done this, there will be both salt and pepper on the
driveway."

Tracks

Tina is walking with Grandma and Granddad in the woods. It is fresh autumn weather and Granddad is walking briskly ahead of them. Tina is taking her time. She sees things of interest everywhere. She puts acorns and chestnuts in a big plastic bag. But there are other things she cannot put in the bag, such as tracks. The sandy ground of the wood is covered in all kinds of tracks, including deer, birds and rabbits. Tina finds the tracks of a deer. Then she is suddenly scared. "Help!" she cries out. "A monster's tracks – look, he's got big around feet."

Grandpa looks at what Tina is pointing to and shakes his head.

"That's not a monster's tracks, dear. Those are the hoof marks of a big horse. You've no need to worry. A rider has been along here this morning."

November 14

In the woods

Natalie is certain that there is nothing finer than riding your horse through the woods. You sit nice and high, there's no need to do any walking and you can see everything easily. On top of that, she has ridden this path through the woods so often that she knows every twist and turn. Or perhaps not?

Oh dear, a tree has fallen across the path. Beside it the undergrowth and trees are too dense. Natalie thinks about it. She has two alternatives, turn back – but she does not want to – or jump the tree. But she is a bit scared of jumping the tree. Can her horse do it? Natalie decides to try.

She urges her horse faster and – up! – they clear the tree effortlessly.

Hey, that was fun!

November 15

Strange sheep

In the autumn, a male sheep, or ram, is usually put in the field with the female sheep, or ewes. He makes sure there will be new lambs in the spring. But today a very strange sheep has joined the ewes in the field. He has long legs and a long tail. Although he does have long hair on his neck, he has no thick wool on his body. The sheep find it strange. They bleat softly to make the acquaintance of the strange sheep, but his answer frightens them. "He-ee-ee!" whinnies the sheep.
No, think the ewes, we do not want any lambs from such a strange ram.

November 16

Raking up the leaves

There are tall trees at the side of the meadow. In the summer, the leaves give splendid shade so that Crispen the pony does not have to stand in the strong sun. But now all the leaves have fallen to the ground. That's why Billy and his father are raking them up. They work all morning. They rake all the leaves into a huge heap. Now they have gone to get the wheelbarrow. Crispen has been watching them from a distance. What are Billy and his father doing? He decides to take a look. Ge-de-dunk, ge-de-dunk! Here he comes at a gallop. Oh dear!
He gallops right through the heap of leaves.
Now Billy and his father must rake them all up again.

November 17

Knights

Imagine
It is long, long ago.
There are no cars
Nor apartments in the towns.

This era, centuries past,
Is called the Middle Ages.
Knights who rode upon their steeds
Were strong and brave as lions.

The true knights lived
In castles large and grand
And just to help them pass the time
They jousted.

November 18

Changing places

Today is the big day. Jasper is nervous. Today he is to participate in the jousting tournament for knights, in which the knights do battle with each other. The object is to knock one of the two knights off his horse. They charge at each other with long poles called lances. This is dangerous, of course. That is why all the knights wear protective metal armor. Jasper is also encased in metal. He does not like it much. It is barely possible to move in such armor. His horse, Guinevere, has the better deal, he believes.

Her entire body is covered with red cloth with golden borders. Her head is covered with a hood with holes for her eyes and ears. She looks magnificent.

"Can't we change places, Guinevere?"

Jasper sighs. "Fine by me," whinnies Guinevere.

"Provided I can ride on your back."

November 19

Black knight

The tournament has begun. Many
knights have been pushed off their
horses. There are now only two
remaining: Jasper and the black
knight. The black knight is quite
fearsome. His horse is black and it
also has a black cloth on its back.
"Ahem," snorts Guinevere, the
mount of Jasper. "He looks like he
is dressed for a funeral." Guinevere
is not frightened by the black
knight. But Jasper is petrified.
"Come on, Jasper!" Guinevere
snorts. "Let's see whose funeral
he's going to – ours or his."

November 20

Reward

It is so exciting. Which knight will win the tournament? Jasper or the black
knight? The horses are thundering toward each other. The knights hold their
lances ready. Both are determined to push the other from his horse. Ge-de-
dunk, ge-de-dunk – they close in on each other.
And then, there is a dull thud and dust flies in the air. When the cloud of dust
clears, one of the knights is on the ground – it is the black knight! Hooray,
Jasper has won! He is rewarded with a kiss from a fair young lady.
"What about me?" Guinevere asks her master.
"Haven't I earned a reward too?"
Of course she has. There is a huge bucket filled with oats in her stall.

Pirate

There is a new pony at the riding school stables called Pirate. The children at the stables are all talking about him. "Who is going to ride him?" they wonder. They are just a little bit scared. A pony called Pirate must not be very good natured. The riding instructor laughs at them.

"Elspeth may ride Pirate. She has nothing to be scared of. He is a very good pony. When you see him, you'll understand why he is called Pirate," she tells them.

Elspeth walks to Pirate's box. Relieved, she sees that Pirate has a black patch around his left eye. It looks just like the eye patch that pirates wear.

"Come on, Pirate," she says to him. "We are going to do well in the class."

November 22

Village festival

There is a festival in the village every year on November 22. There are stalls on the village square filled with lots of tasty things to buy. All the adults come there to enjoy each other's company and to listen to the music. The children play games. Mark drags his mother with him to the corner of the square. There are a couple of ponies there.

For fifty cents he can ride around the square. Clip, clop, clip – there goes Mark on a pony. But once around the square is not enough for Mark. They are soon back. Disappointed, Mark climbs down.

There is another child waiting.

"If you are good, you can have another turn soon," his mother promises.

November 23

Cart

There is an advertisement for a pony cart in the newspaper.
"Hey, what about it? Shall we get a cart for your pony?" Angela's father asks her.
"Then the family can go out together." Angela looks glum. She much prefers
riding her pony alone. A stupid cart – that is nothing for her. But her father has
made up his mind. He calls the person immediately to ask if the cart is still for
sale. Shortly afterward, Angela dives into the stable. She grumbles to her pony.
"I'm warning you. Soon you must pull this wretched cart. Be really naughty and
then Daddy will give up the idea."
It is just as well that Angela's pony cannot understand what she says.

November 24

Quite fun

"Ugh! I hate it!" Angela hisses through
her teeth. She is being taught to drive a
pony and cart. She has to hold the reins
in one hand and the whip in the other.
With her tongue stuck out, she struggles
to master it. After lots of practice, she
can cope. Then she has her first real
lesson driving the cart. Mother and
Father and her sister are in the back of
the cart.
"Walk on!" Angela says, clicking her
tongue. They are off. All along the road
people stop to stare and admire them.
"Good day!" She waves cheerfully.
Angela feels like the king of the castle.
The cart is much better than she
imagined – especially when she is
driving.

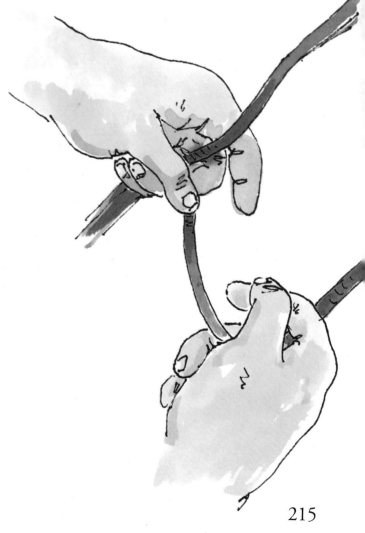

Trouble with the neighbors

Tara has trouble with her neighbors. They are eating her food. Perhaps you think neighbors wouldn't do that. But Tara's neighbors are mice. They have made a home in the horse's stall. It is pleasantly warm there and there is plenty to eat. When Tara eats her oats, the mice gnaw at her hay. When she eats her hay, they start on her oats.

"I've had enough of this!" thinks Tara. "Those wretched mice are now sitting in my feed box." Quietly she slips up to her box and picks up one of the mice by its tail.

"Squeak, squeak," cries the mouse. "You're much bigger than the cat. I'm moving!"

"Thank goodness," mumbles Tara. "Now I can eat in peace."

November 26

Digging

Blaze has discovered how much fun it is to dig. Using a front hoof, he scratches the ground. He has made a large bare patch in the grass. Blaze digs deeper until he has made quite a ditch. Then he drops to his knees and rolls over on his back.
"Aaaah, that's good!" groans Blaze as he rubs his back against the ground. Blaze is very happy with his ditch. But perhaps his owner will not be so happy. A ditch in the meadow and a horse covered with dirt is not everyone's idea of fun.

November 27

Deaf

Horses have good hearing, much better than people. Yet some horses are deaf. Bertie is such a horse.
"But Bertie is still the best horse," explains Nick, his rider. "He is not frightened by sudden noises because he cannot hear them." But surely Bertie must be surprised by Nick if he cannot hear him approaching? Not at all! There is nothing wrong with Bertie's eyes and he probably has a better sense of smell than other horses. Sometimes Nick gets a bit annoyed with his horse and he says: "Stupid creature."
Fortunately, Bertie cannot hear him say it.

November 28

Bed

Caroline is staying at her uncle and aunt's farm. They have lots of animals: cows, chickens, pigs, but also a horse called Ben.
"Come on, Caroline," says her uncle that evening. "Let's put the horse to bed." They walk to the horse's stable. Uncle tells her: "You get his bed ready and I will collect him from the field." When her uncle comes back, Caroline is sitting, crying, on a bale of straw.
"I couldn't find his sheets and mattress anywhere," she sniffles. Uncle laughs. "You didn't look hard enough. You are sitting on his mattress. Ben lies on a thick bed of straw."

November 29

Awake

"Mommy!" little Edward calls from his bed. Mother comes to see what is up.
"What's the matter, darling?"
"I can't sleep."
"But it's nine o'clock. If you don't sleep you will be too tired to play tomorrow," says his mother.
"I know, but I just can't sleep," sighs Edward.
"Then you must think of something nice," suggests Mommy. "What do you like?"
"Horses!" says Edward.
"Then think very carefully about your favorite horse and I will sing you a lullaby," Mommy promises.
She starts to sing:
"Sleep, Edward, sleep. Outside trots a horse…" Before the song is finished, Edward is snoring.

November 30

Lullaby

Sleep, little Edward, slumber
Hooves of horses thunder.
A horse with flowing mane
Peeps through the windowpane
Sleep, little Edward, slumber
Hooves of horses thunder.

December 1

Fast sleigh

The winters in faraway Russia are very severe. In December, there is already a thick layer of snow on the fields. This is why people travel by horse-drawn sleighs. Boris has a fast sleigh and an even quicker horse. His neighbor Ivan does not like this. Ivan wants to be the fastest. He tries everything. He gives his horse extra feed but Boris is still faster. Ivan strips his sleigh to make it as light as possible, but Boris is still faster.
"Mmm," complains Ivan jealously.
"There must be a way that I can go quicker."

December 2

Three against one

"Hey, Boris, shall we have a race?" calls Ivan to his neighbor. "Let's see who has the fastest sleigh."
Boris is surprised. He knows that his horse is the fastest sleigh horse in the area. Does Ivan never learn? But when Boris sees Ivan's sleigh he understands. Ivan has adapted his sleigh. Now it can be drawn by three horses.
"That's not fair!" shouts Boris angrily. "Three against one is cheating!" Ivan does not mind if Boris is angry. He just wants to be the fastest for once.
"Ready to go? Go!" Ivan shoots away. Boris has to admit that three horses pulling a sleigh is a magnificent sight.

December 3

Sharing

Sharing everything fairly
Is what you do with friends
Even when they snort and whinny
And have two more legs than me.

Sandwiches and my apple
You munch up happily
But what for me is quite enough
Is a mere light snack for you.

December 4

Equal shares

Every Monday, Geraldine goes straight from school to the riding stable wearing her riding breeches and boots. Fortunately, the stable is close to the school. It means she has time to eat and drink something before the lesson. Her mother always puts some tasty cake and an apple in her bag. The cake Geraldine eats herself. She eats half the apple. The other half she gives to her favorite pony, Aster. Aster knows that Geraldine is coming. She is waiting for her. Every Monday she gets half an apple from Geraldine.
Aster likes Geraldine.

December 5

Boots

Freddie the stable boy is being called. He must go quickly.
"Darn it!" complains Freddie. "I'm in the middle of mucking out a stall. My clothes are filthy and my boots too."
Grumpily he changes rapidly but, in his haste, he leaves a boot in the stable.
"Hey!" sniffs Coco the horse. "What's that on the ground?" It smells of Freddie, but with the added aroma of cheesy feet." Coco bites the boot and tosses it about.
"Boring!" thinks Coco. "A boot isn't much fun to play with and you can't eat it. I'd rather have an apple."

December 6

Too small

Peter's little sister is a bit jealous. Her big brother goes riding, but she is too small.
"Not fair," she says. Peter sympathizes with his sister.
"I tell you what," he says, "Today I will be your horse."
Peter drops to his hands and knees and crawls. His little sister may climb onto his back.
"This is fun!" His little sister shrieks with pleasure. Peter is very careful of his sister on his back, but she is not so careful. She pulls Peter's hair and kicks her heels into him.
"Now I understand why you are too young to ride a horse," moans Peter.

December 7

Sugar cubes

Karen has a big bag of sugar cubes. She wants to give them to the horses. She thinks the horses will find them tasty.

"Hey! What are you doing?" she hears suddenly. It is the owner of the horses. "Don't you know that sugar is very bad for their teeth?"

Oh dear, Karen had not thought of that. She blushes bright pink in shame. The owner sees that Karen did not mean any harm. He says, "Come with me. It is feeding time. You can help me give the horses their oats and hay. That is much healthier for them."

December 8

Snow horse

It has snowed. When David gets out of bed, he knows right away what he will do today: make a snowman. He goes out immediately after breakfast. He picks up an armful of snow and starts to work. An hour later, his mother comes to see what he has done.

"Is it going okay, David?" she asks. David nods. He has rosy flushed cheeks from the hard work. Mother has an idea. "Would you like a carrot for the nose?" David shakes. Mother does not understand. "Why not?" David sighs. "Because I am making a snow horse, not a snowman. A horse big enough to sit on." Mother understands now. A horse with a carrot for its nose would not look right.

December 9

Escaped

Megan is bored in her stable. She plucks at some hay with her lips. She looks out of the small window and rubs against the wall.

"Bah!" grumbles Megan. "I want to go outside. There is nothing to do in the stable." She walks over to the stable door to look at the bolt. "What an invention," she sighs. "Just the sort of thing humans would think up." She thinks about it for some time. How does her owner open the door? To open the door, he slides the bolt. Megan tries doing so. After half an hour of trying, she moves the bolt. Suddenly the door opens.

Dear me, Megan has escaped!

December 10

Back

Megan managed to escape from her boring stable. Happily she trots along the path. She passes along a sand track and through a field.

"Fantastic!" she whinnies to the birds. "Great!" she calls to the trees. "Wonderful," she sighs to the sheep. Without noticing, Megan has lost her way. Then it begins to snow, at first gently and then much harder with bigger flakes.

"Brr!" shivers Megan. She is getting very cold. She is also getting wetter. She wants to be back in her stable. "I'll never run away again," Megan promises.

Hedgehog

"Mom, I'm going with Zoe to see Hedgehog," Hilary tells her mother when they come out of school. Mother looks somewhat surprised. "That's a bit strange, isn't it? Hedgehogs hibernate through the winter. You won't see one in December."

Hilary laughs. "I didn't say I was going to look at a hedgehog but at *Hedgehog*. That's the name of Zoe's pony. Zoe has clipped his mane so that it sticks up like a hedgehog."

Now her mother understands. "I hope Zoe's Hedgehog does not hibernate," she jokes.

December 12

Snowballs

Andrew goes to see his pony. He is a sturdy Icelandic pony well able to withstand the cold. But Andrew still worries about him. There is a thick covering of snow. Will Hagar be able to find enough to eat?

"Hagar! Hagar!" Andrew calls. Here he comes at full gallop. He scrunches to a halt, throwing snow into the air. Andrew is covered in it.

"Oh!" cries Andrew. "So you want to play with snowballs, do you? Just you wait!" He makes a snowball and throws it at Hagar. At first, the pony is frightened, but he catches the next snowball in his mouth.

"Hagar, champion snowball eater!" laughs Andrew.

December 13

Fox hunting

Today the horses are able to go out into the field. They enjoy that. They canter and play and when it is time to go back to their stable, none of them want to. The owner has three men to help him around them up. Puffing and panting, the men have finally managed to get almost all of them back in their stalls. All except a chestnut.
"He-ee-ee!" whinnies Little Fox. "Catch me if you can!" The men chase the pony for at least an hour. He keeps escaping from them until finally they catch him.
"Phew!" puffs the owner. "That was a real fox hunt."

December 14

Jack Frost

"Hey, what are they?" whinnies Bonny one morning. She cannot see out of her stable window. It looks as though there are flowers stuck to it.
"Mmm! Flowers." She smacks her lips. You don't see many during the winter." She tries to lick the flowers with her tongue. But they are on the outside of the window and they are very cold. Bonny does not know about Jack Frost – how he paints pretty pictures that evaporate if a horse's warm tongue licks them. Surprised, she sees that the flowers are disappearing.
"Oh well," she sighs. "You wouldn't get very fat from such flowers anyway."

Busby

In ten more days, it will be Christmas. In the houses of the village, there are lots of Christmas trees. It is now time to put up the big tree in the village square. The men have already selected one in the forest. They fell it carefully. Now it has to be taken to the village. That is work for Busby.
Busby is a huge, strong farm horse. The tree is attached to his harness by chains. The tree is very heavy. Will Busby be able to pull it?

December 16

Worthy

Busby puffs and sweats. "What a job!" Busby is pulling the huge pine tree from the forest to the village. He strains all his muscles because the tree is so heavy. It starts to snow. Busby wants to quit, but then he notices that the tree slides more easily over the snow.
"Heave, heave!" snorts Busby. "We're almost there."
Yes, there is the village square. That is where the tree will stand. Busby has done his work well. His owner slaps his neck in a friendly way.
"You're a worthy horse. We'd never have managed without you. Now you can go back to your stable. Tomorrow I'll let you see the decorated tree."

228

December 17

Apples?

Busby tells the other horses in the stables about the Christmas tree in the village square. "It is beautiful and decorated all over with colored lights," he tells them. "And the people have hung all sorts of things all over it."
"What sort of things?" Conker asks.
"I'm not sure," admits Busby. "They looked like balls and were around and shiny."
Conker thinks about it. "Perhaps they were apples." Conker licks his lips at the thought of a tree hung with hundreds of juicy apples.
Busby shakes his head. "I don't think so. At least, I've never seen purple and silver apples."

December 18

Christmas tree for horses

Horses are not dumb at all
In fact, they're rather clever.
Imagine how a horse would choose
To decorate a Christmas tree.
No tinsel or silly baubles
But a tree loaded with carrots
Apples, sugar lumps and mints
All of which are edible,
But that's not the whole story,
Says Conker with a grin.
"These colors are quite suited
To the green of a Christmas tree."

December 19

Reindeer

Of course you know that Santa
Claus's sleigh is pulled by reindeer.
The male reindeer have large antlers
with a soft covering like velvet. A
horse has no ideas what a reindeer
is. Drakar the big stallion is getting
quite annoyed.
"Why don't they use horses to pull
Santa Claus's sleigh?" he mutters.
"Horses can gallop far faster than
reindeer."

December 20

Summer horse

Some horses can withstand cold weather. They grow a long, thick winter coat
that protects them. They even enjoy the snow and ice. But Ayesha detests the
winter. She is an Arab. And Arabs are desert horses that can withstand the heat.
Even with a thick blanket, Ayesha is shivering. "Oh, I wish it was summer
again," she sighs. "I hate the winter. I'm a real summer horse."

December 21

Fright

A stranger comes to the door. He has seen Carl's pony in the field.
"That's a lovely pony," says the man. "Do you want to sell him?"
Carl is shocked beyond belief.
"Absolutely not," he says, shaking his head vehemently. "My pony is not for sale." The thought alone upsets Carl. He could not bear to be parted from his pony.
The man sees that Carl has gone white as a sheet.
"Don't be afraid," the man says soothingly. "You obviously love your pony and I won't ask again to buy him from you. You look after him really well."

December 22

Salt

Caramba the mare looks up. Who is this coming into her stall? Oh, it is Phillipa, her owner. She is carrying something. Phillipa has a large block. She hangs it up in Caramba's box. Curious, Caramba sniffs it. "Can you eat it?" she asks herself. Hesitantly, she takes a lick. Mmm – it tastes salty. Phillipa strokes Caramba's mane.
"That is a salt block," she explains.
"There are also vitamins in it. It is good for you." Caramba likes a bit of salt.
"But you get rather thirsty!" he whinnies.

Donkey

At the Christmas market in the square
Are all kinds of stalls filled with wares.
But the finest one – and that's no fib –
Is a full-size stable with its crib.
Shepherds and their flock abiding,
But in the corner a donkey's hiding,
Hoping you can't see or hear –
He's so embarrassed by his ears.

December 24

Laughingstock

Sooty the pony is very angry. He has to play the part of the donkey in the Nativity scene. Sooty does not want to.

"I am a pony, not a stupid donkey!" complains Sooty. "And to make matters worse, they have stuck these stupid, long paper ears on me. I am a laughingstock."

This is why Sooty is hiding at the back of the Nativity scene. So nobody can see him. Angrily he tries to shake the stupid ears from his head. He shakes so hard that an ear really does fly off. The ear hangs next to Sooty's cheek.

"Ha ha," laugh the sheep.

"Silly Sooty," moos the ox.

"I don't care," mutters Sooty. "At least everybody can see that I am not a donkey."

December 25

Bells

"Ding-dong," ring the church bells. It is Christmas Day. Today the people celebrate the birth of baby Jesus. People come from near and far to the church. Some come by car and others walk. But what is that? Suddenly there is a cheerful sound of jingling bells. Here comes a sleigh drawn by a beautiful horse. The harness of the horse has lots of little silver bells on it. As he trots, they all tinkle.

"Ting-a-ling, ting-a-ling," they say. "Merry Christmas, everyone!"

233

December 26

Presents

There are still presents under the Christmas tree. Karen and Michael opened their presents from Mommy and Daddy yesterday, but today other members of the family are coming to lunch. Some of the presents are for aunts and uncles, but Karen and Michael know that there are also presents for them still under the tree.

Now that Grandma and Granddad have arrived, they are finally allowed to open their other presents. When they have ripped all the paper off the presents with their names on, there is still another package. Who is it for? Karen reads the label. In large letters it says: "For Jubilee."

"That's nice!" cries Karen, "Santa Claus has not forgotten our pony." Michael wants to open the present, but Karen stops him. "No," she says. "We'll take it to the stable and open it there. Jubilee also likes surprises."

December 27

Thanks

Santa Claus has brought a present for Jubilee the horse. Karen and Michael show the package to Jubilee. He does not understand. He has never seen a present. Michael holds the box while Karen opens it. Curiously, the two children and the horse peer into the box.
"Ooh," cries Michael.
"How nice," sighs Karen.
In the box, there is a new harness for Jubilee. It is black leather with shiny, silvery fastenings.
"Thank you, Santa Claus!" cry Michael and Karen.
"He-ee-ee!" whinnies Jubilee.
That surely means "thank you very much" in horse talk.

December 28

Elfin horse

Most zoos and places with animals on display are not worth visiting in winter. All the animals are indoors in their warm quarters. But there is a very unusual animal collection in the town where Jake lives. All the animals are quite happy to be out-of-doors. Jake likes to visit the park where the animals are to be found quite often. He can happily watch the sheep and penguins for hours. But his favorite animals are the miniature ponies.
He calls them "Elfin ponies."
"If I open my eyes just a little," says Jake, "I can imagine elves sitting on their backs. Elves with red pointed hats and white beards."

Dumplings

The Jansen family are visiting relatives in the Netherlands for the Christmas and New Year holidays. Angela is helping Aunt Anneke and cousin Josefien make oliebollen, or oil dumplings. They are fried in oil and then coated in icing sugar. They are as closely associated with New Year celebrations in the Netherlands as plum pudding is with Christmas in Britain. So many dumplings have been made that they have run out of places to cool them. So Aunt Anneke has put some on the windowsill. Unfortunately, the window is open and Josefien's pony, Slimpie, has escaped again. There is a crash as the plate falls off the windowsill and there is Slimpie gobbling up the dumplings. After laughing at the sight, they quickly rush outside to grab the dumplings before the pony eats them all and gets an upset tummy.

"Your pony should be called Dumpling rather than Slimpie," says Angela.

December 30

Cotton wool

Cousin Josefien asks her mother to buy some cotton wool for her pony when she goes shopping.

"Why do you need cotton wool for your pony?" asks Angela with curiosity.

"To make earplugs," says cousin Josefien.

"Earplugs?" wonders Angela.

"At midnight tomorrow almost everybody in the Netherlands will let off fireworks. My pony can't stand all that noise, so I will put earplugs in her ears. Then she can sleep soundly."

December 31

Fireworks

At midnight throughout the country,
The sky is brightly lit
As billions of fireworks
Mark the New Year.

But what a racket
All those rockets make.
A frightened horse asks,
"Do we really need this?"

He folds his ears
Against his neck
And says, cross as two sticks,
"People must be mad!"

"So much money!
Think of all the food
That could buy
For horses everywhere."